12/14

Henderson

WITHDRAWN

D1264996

THE FASHION SWATCH BOOK

MARNIE FOGG

THE FASHION SWATCH BOOK

1,155 ILLUSTRATIONS, 965 IN COLOR

Thames & Hudson

Dedicated to Grace Whitehurst

On the cover: kaleidoscopic hamsa motif all-over print by Yaelle (2013).
Page 1: 'Swan Lake', digital print by Basso & Brooke (S/S 2010).
Pages 2–3: the 'tissue' side of frayed jacquard fragments in silk and lamé, from Stephen Walters and Sons.
This page: files of swatch books at Giles, stored beneath Pac-Man-inspired helmets.

The Fashion Swatch Book © 2014 Thames & Hudson Ltd, London
Text © 2014 Marnie Fogg
Images © 2014 the individual contributors

Designed by Tz Rallis

First published in 2014 in paperback in the United States of America by Thames & Hudson Inc., 500 Fifth Avenue, New York, New York 10110

thamesandhudsonusa.com

Library of Congress Catalog Card Number 2013948279

ISBN 978-0-500-29133-7

Printed and bound in China by
C&C Offset Printing Co., Ltd.

CONTENTS

An asterisk (*) after the name of a designer or company denotes that they also appear in The Techniques, pages 378–429.

THE TECHNIQUES:

INTRODUCTION

Without fabric there would be no fashion. Whether woven, knitted, printed, embroidered or bejewelled, textiles are crucial to the eloquence of apparel and fundamental to the fashion design process. *The Fashion Swatch Book* features a diverse collection of more than a thousand swatch samples of textiles garnered from the studios of cutting-edge contemporary designers and from the luxury heritage labels that manufacture their own woven silks or knitted cashmere.

Traditionally, the swatch or pattern book is a seasonal record of a manufacturer's output, consisting of a swatch (cutting of fabric) with production notes alongside it for future reference. It provides not only an invaluable record of the manufacturing and design process but also a source of future inspiration. *The Fashion Swatch Book* addresses all aspects of textiles for fashion, and it is not limited to those by a single designer or manufacturer. It also encompasses textiles for fashion in which the surface decoration of a single swatch is the result of a variety of techniques and treatments.

After a millennium of development and refinement, from the emergence of the weavers' guilds in the 11th century to the mechanization of the print process at the beginning of the 20th century, the precisely programmed special effects of new technologies are now emerging. They have modernized and liberated many traditional craft processes: looms have become highly automated and computer-driven technology enables manufacturers to customize a particular effect and to produce short runs of specially commissioned cloth, outputting bespoke, extraordinary and spectacular fabrics that fuel the designers' creativity and provide an industry with artisanal elegance. This level of digital precision and technical virtuosity underpins the use of modern craft practices, such as ultrasound welding, esoteric engineering methods, digital printing and seamless knitting processes. These methods occasionally usurp, but do not replace, the *plumassiers* (feather workers), bead workers and leather workers of the *atelier* (workshop), or the *petites mains* (literally, 'little hands') of haute couture, who sustain the couturiers' art. This is demonstrated at Maison Vermont, which was acquired by luxe couture house Christian Dior in 2012 and is dedicated to hand embroidery.

When the screen-printing process was patented by Samuel Simon in 1907, the invention became instrumental in providing the market with the first fashion fabrics in bulk. This relatively cheap and less laborious method of printing cloth accelerated the speed of response to changing fashion trends and liberated designers from the limitations of expensive block-printing methods and engraved roller machines. Digital printing has further democratized the print process. Taking an image directly from a camera or computer screen to the cloth in one step means that countless colour separations are eliminated. However, there are a number of designers whose engagement with the

John Smedley swatch sample cards of stripes and intarsia Argyle checks.

'Guard' books from Stephen Walters and
Sons record all the technical information
needed to replicate the designs.

A record of small-scale jacquard
designs for use as tie fabrics,
from Stephen Walters and Sons.

digital process goes far beyond the
convenience of short runs and nullified
screen costs. The process is now a new
medium in its own right, seen in the digital
prints of Basso & Brooke and Peter Jensen.
Furthermore, digital prints are often enriched
with 21st-century effects, including laser-
cutting and traditional beaded embellishment,
utilized by contemporary designers such
as Mary Katrantzou, whose maximalist
aesthetic combines tin cans and tropical fish,
and recreations of Fabergé eggs as wearable
art. Holly Fulton's penchant for Art Deco and
Louise Gray's anarchic quirkiness epitomize
the innovation-led experimentation with
surfaces and colour.

The traditional craft of hand-knitting
continues to be used by designers such as
Carlo Volpi, who subverts the traditional
nature of the medium to produce large-scale
innovative textures. In 1589, the knitting
process was mechanized by William Lee
of Nottinghamshire, who invented the
stocking frame; since the 1970s, automated,
electronically controlled knitting machines
have grown to dominate the market in
tandem with the accelerated evolution of
information technology in general. Machine
builders, such as Stoll of Germany and Shima
Seiki of Japan, vie in the global market to
provide the most sophisticated CAD/CAM
design systems and the most versatile and
productive machine types. These enable
the free configuration of rich patterns,
complex structures and garment shapes,
as well as a rapid turnaround between styles.
Similarly, electronic control with individual
needle selection has facilitated quick
response manufacturing of unprecedented
patterning and shaping that previously could
be attained only by labour-intensive and
expensive manual processes.

Changing something as simple as
the coloration of a design can render
an archive textile contemporary.

The 'Guard' books contain an archive
of every design produced by Stephen
Walters and Sons from the 18th century.

In the pursuit of an intensely focused aesthetic, some fabric companies have sustained the highest levels of manual precision and reverence for artisanal methods, harnessed with advanced technology. The Nuno Corporation, founded in Japan by Junichi Arai, is seen as a role model in the contemporary craft renaissance that hybridizes painstaking traditions with modern innovations. Fashion and fabric also speak in eloquent counterpoint with the bespoke confections of Bruce Oldfield and the unsurpassed textiles of Forster Rohner, supplied to an 'A' list of couture houses and designers including Valentino and Erdem. Many fashion designers and brands also depend upon textile creatives such as Lewis & Lewis Design and The Colorfield for the promulgation of their label.

As modern life becomes increasingly dominated by technology, provenance and authenticity accrue greater resonance. Great European and US fashion houses, including Oscar de la Renta, Jean Paul Gaultier, Hermès and Louis Vuitton, now use Britain's heritage manufacturers for their lace, tweed and cashmere, attracted by the authenticity of the product, the small production runs and an acute attention to detail. The fine woollen mills of northern England have existed since the Industrial Revolution and they now provide cloth for international designers. Similarly, Scottish tweed and cashmere manufacturers export their textiles worldwide: Johnstons of Elgin has a manufacturing base both in north-east Scotland and in the Scottish Borders, where the indigenous water of the River Teviot is instrumental in the resulting softness of the yarn. William Linton's soft lightweight tweeds, developed in 1912 as a contrast to the traditional rural ruggedness of Scottish

John Smedley sample
colour swatch card.

Various colourways of printed
foulard designs from Paul Smith.

tweeds, were used by Coco Chanel in 1928 and were the foundation of the couturier's iconic bouclé suits in her comeback collection of 1954. There is also a recent revival of tweeds on the catwalk, and Johnstons continues to offer a bespoke service to designers such as Ralph Lauren and Victoria Beckham. A number of other long-established manufacturers, such as Suffolk silk weavers Stephen Walters and Sons, collaborate with British designers Jonathan Saunders and Giles Deacon, while Nottinghamshire company Cluny Lace – the only Leavers lace factory remaining in the UK – services major international designers including Vivienne Westwood and Dolce & Gabbana.

Garments made with labour-intensive methods and rare fibres have always been the prerogative of persons of a high social status, such as the aristocracy and royalty. Driven by the notion of luxuriousness and exclusivity,

the global textile trade – originating in the 1st century BCE with the links between the Far and Middle East and Europe – established a geographical textile map that still exists today. One centre of excellence is Como in Italy, which continues to have Europe's largest concentration of silk manufacturers and printers. Its reputation was first established around 1400, when Ludovico Sforza, the Duke of Milan, imposed on farmers the mandatory cultivation of mulberry trees – essential for the breeding of the silk worm. Merino sheep still graze on the foothills of the Snowy Mountains of Australia's New South Wales, from where their fine wool is shipped to the oldest of England's knitwear manufacturers, John Smedley. In Macclesfield, England's historical centre of silk production, R. A. Smart was instrumental in bringing digital-printing methods to the attention of contemporary designers. Today the company maintains

Bruce Oldfield's garment design sketches with corresponding swatch samples.

Rolls of printed fabric designs by the metre from Alexander Henry Fabrics.

a well-established reputation as the protagonist for textile innovation and new printing systems. Fine goldwork is found only at London-based company Hand & Lock and the embroidery house is the go-to place for rich adornments, bespoke embroidery and authentic crests, such as the one worked for the Burberry Prorsum label.

A major subtext to the increasing significance of fabric development and diversification within the entire machinery of the fashion industry is the overwhelming contemporary importance of online media and sales. It is now common for key designers to produce exclusive ranges for major fashion portals, such as Net-A-Porter and Moda Operandi. Within this commercial environment, the continual refreshment of stock with new lines is pivotal to the maintenance of browsing and shopping appetites. Decorative fabrics are critical to evidencing change and, well beyond traditional seasonal changes, they are more important now than at any other time in the history of post-industrial fashion commerce. Contemporary designers such as House of Holland and James Long are liberated by the accessibility of bespoke hand and digital processes and can multiply their output within their signature style using a constant refreshment of fabric identity.

The Fashion Swatch Book concludes with a glossary of fabrics and techniques, and an anthology of black-and-white images that offer a detailed and sequential technical overview of a number of processes from a range of manufacturing environments. These provide information on appropriate materials, construction methods and finishing processes, thus enabling the potential designer to contextualize the techniques within their design practice.

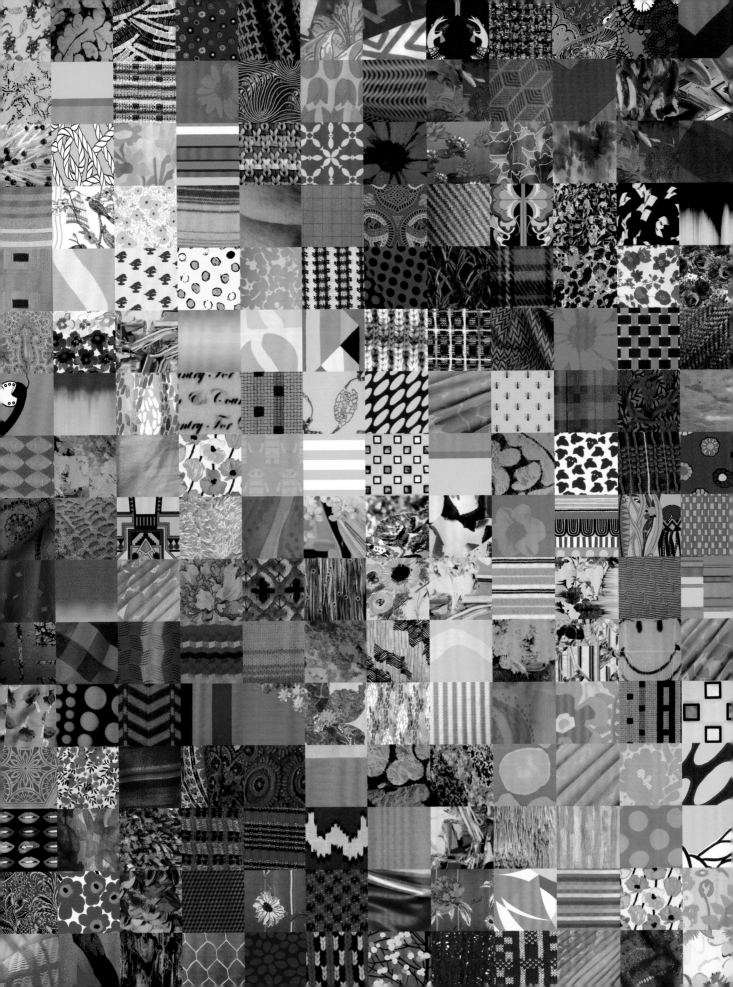

ALEXANDER HENRY FABRICS

Located in Burbank, California, the premier fabric design house Alexander Henry produces original cotton prints under the direction of the family-run De Leon Design Group: Marc, Phillip and Nicole de Leon. The textiles encompass a wide range of designs inspired by multifarious subjects, from popular culture to art history, and they are grouped into specific seasonal themes that appear in the biannual collections. The company has distributors in Canada, Australia and Europe, as well as in Japan, where most of the printing takes place. With designs featured in the New York Textile Museum, the company sells prints to a diverse range of clients, from cutting-edge designers to large corporate manufacturers around the world, for use in the clothing, accessories and home furnishings industries.

THE STUDIO PROCESS

Alexander Henry fabrics are resolutely grounded in the traditional design process of printed textiles. The in-house team of artists paints each pattern by hand, using primarily watercolour, luma dye and gouache, in a process that lends a unique quality to the prints and an intimacy to the finished product.

01. *'Urban Garden' from the* Mecca For Modern *collection (S/S 2013).*
02. *'Mwamba Abstract' from the* Africa *collection (S/S 2013).*
03. *'Camelia' from the* Black and White *collection (S/S 2010).*

following pages
04. *'Sloane' from the* Fulham Road *collection (S/S 2013).*
05. *'Larkspur In Bloom' from the* Larkspur *collection (A/W 2011).*
06. *'Jardin de San Marcos' from the* Folklorico *collection (A/W 2011).*
07. *'Mocca' from the* Fashionista *collection (A/W 2003).*
08. *'Trios' from the* Fulham Road Lawn *collection (A/W 2010).*

01

04

14
→15

16

DIRECTIONAL PRINTS

The hand of the artist is evident in the idiosyncratic line and quirky detailing of these directional prints. In each, the design reads either vertically or horizontally across the cloth, which is deployed accordingly.

previous pages
09. *'Strawberry' from the* Nicole's Prints *collection (S/S 2003).*
10. *'Zahara' from the* Africa *collection (S/S 2013).*
11. *'Holland' from the* In The Kitchen *collection (S/S 2009).*
12. *'Farmdale Orchard' from the* In The Kitchen *collection (A/W 2010).*
13. *'Masara' from the* Exotica *collection (S/S 2013).*

this page
14. *'Keely' from the* AH Fashion for Home *collection (S/S 2013).*
15. *'Keely' from the* AH Fashion for Home *collection (S/S 2013).*
16. *'Keely' from the* AH Fashion for Home *collection (S/S 2013).*
17. *'June Bug' from the* June Bug *collection (A/W 2011).*
18. *'Larkspur Meadow' from the* Larkspur *collection (A/W 2011).*
19. *'Larkspur' from the* Larkspur *collection (A/W 2011).*

ALTUZARRA

Merging his Parisian roots with a New York sensibility of urban luxury ready-to-wear fashion, Joseph Altuzarra creates distinct pieces of sharp tailoring and body-defining dresses with a modern edge. After interning at Marc Jacobs and working as a freelance designer for New York-based label Proenza Schouler, Altuzarra apprenticed with patternmaker Nicolas Caïto, former head of the Rochas atelier, to further hone his technical skills. The designer returned to Paris in 2006, working as first assistant to Riccardo Tisci at Givenchy. Altuzarra launched his eponymous label in New York in 2008 with a debut collection of fifteen pieces and has since won a number of prestigious awards.

IKAT WEAVING
Altuzarra introduces the feather effect of ikat weaving (**03**), in which the warp or weft, or both, is tie-dyed in the Rastafarian colours of red, yellow and green.

01. *Digital print of cutwork clothes and lace pattern collages together on a chambray base (Resort 2014).*
02. *Loose cotton knit in Rastafarian colourways (S/S 2013).*
03. *Digital print inspired by the abstract shapes featured in Bob Winston's* Silver Bracelet with Nest and Three Brass Eggs and Large Turquoise Stone *(1948) (S/S 2013).*

04. *Digitally printed plaid on a fil coupé fabric (A/W 2011).*
05. *Pleated and crinkled chiffons clustered and stitched together to give a feather-like appearance (Resort 2014).*
06. *Gold metal sequins hand embroidered with red thread onto a printed ikat crêpe de Chine fabric in hues of indigo blue (Resort 2013).*
07. *Printed faux ikat woven cloth with mirrored image (Resort 2013).*

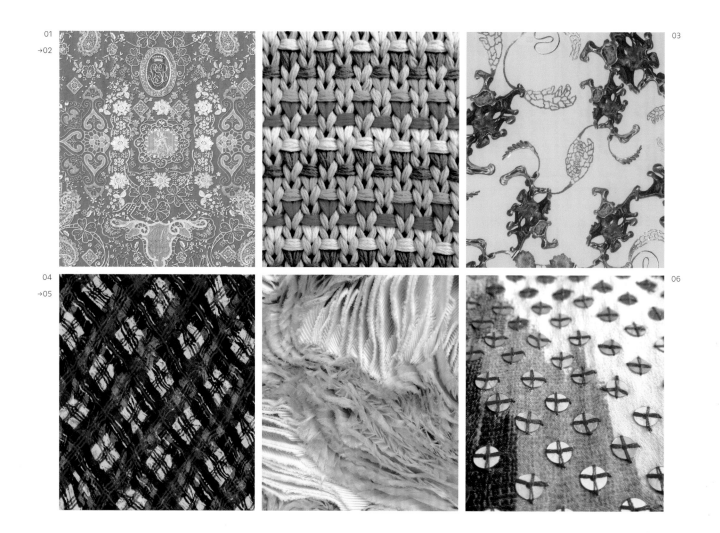

01
→02

03

04
→05

06

08

08. *Handmade brass metal fringe tassels, metal thread and sequin starbursts on silk charmeuse (S/S 2013).*

09. *Metallic gold thread embroidery in a classic Romanian pattern (Resort 2014).*

10. *Gold stacks of sequins and small glass beads arranged to create an oversized snake pattern (Resort 2014).*

11. *Brass bead cross embroidery with Swarouski crystal centres (S/S 2013).*

12. *Metal thread and sequin starbursts on charmeuse, brass teardrop fan embroidery on cotton canvas and Swarouski crystals in brass settings on cotton (S/S 2013).*

ANN LOUISE ROSWALD

Based in London, Ann Louise Roswald pursues a traditional approach to fabric embellishment, employing processes such as screen-printing for her signature floral prints and also practising long-held embroidery techniques such as tambour beading. The designer invariably references the natural world in her search for inspiration. Roswald launched her own line in London store Liberty in 1998. The internationally recognized label has showrooms in Düsseldorf and Munich in Germany and exhibits collections seasonally in London, Paris and New York. Exquisite fabrics form the basis of the collections and Roswald works with highly innovative textile manufacturers in France to develop exclusive jacquard weaves based on her print designs, while tweeds are produced in Scotland.

ELECTRONIC PATTERNING PRODUCTION

Roswald's fabrics can be defined by the opulent surfaces she produces by hand methods. There are further materials that maintain this richness of texture and colour by exploiting digital jacquard weaving and electronic jersey production.

01. *Two-colour jacquard weave (A/W 2012).*
02. *Three-colour double jersey with inlay (A/W 2012).*
03. *Two-colour figured jersey (A/W 2012).*
04. *Tambour beading on a knit base in merino wool. The knitted fabric is also used to cover the domed beads. The thread is wrapped around metal rings to create the centre of the flower motif (A/W 2012).*

01
→02

03

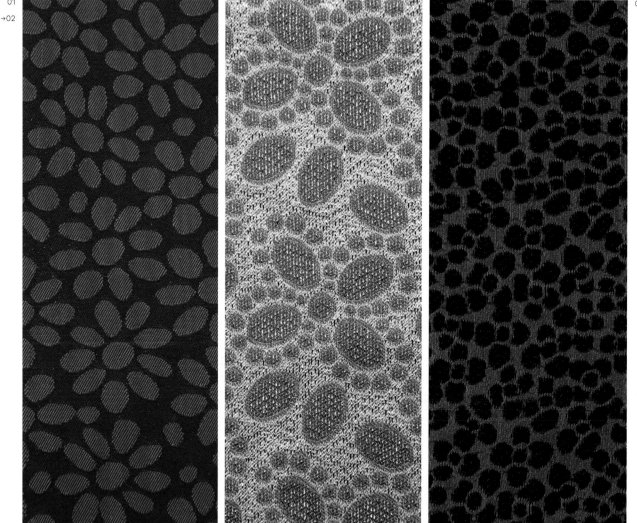

TAMBOUR BEADING

Ann Louise Roswald incorporates fabric embellishment alongside the traditional technique of tambour beading to produce intricately textured surfaces. These are fashioned into simple graphic silhouettes that characterize the designer's pared-down tailoring and understated garments.

05. *Tambour beading using sequins (S/S 2012).*

06. *Tambour beading using sequins and strips of pleated silk satin, with domed beads covered in silk satin (A/W 2011).*

07. *Silk satin pleated embroidery with crystals and large metal sequins (S/S 2010).*

08. *Tambour beading using sequins (S/S 2012).*

09. *Tambour beading using sequins and strips of pleated silk satin, with domed beads covered in silk satin (A/W 2011).*

10. *Silk satin pleated embroidery with crystals and large metal sequins (S/S 2010).*

11. *Tambour beading using sequins and strips of pleated silk satin with covered domed beads (S/S 2012).*

05
→06

07

08
→09

10

13

14

15

16

SCREEN-PRINTING

Ann Louise Roswald's nature-inspired print designs are handcrafted using screen-printing techniques. The bold prints of strong graphic shapes are used for entire garments, as smaller details or as coat linings.

12. *Printed silk crêpe 'Leaf' in geranium (A/W 2011).*
13. *Printed silk satin 'Pansy' in parfait (S/S 2011).*
14. *Printed silk satin 'Geometric Leaf' in pewter (A/W 2008).*
15. *Silk jacquard weave 'Daisy Stripe' in gold (A/W 2009).*
16. *Printed silk jersey 'Bold Leaf' in chartreuse (S/S 2011).*

ANTIK BATIK

The bohemian eclecticism of the Antik Batik label is fuelled by the global travels of designer Gabriella Cortese. At the age of eighteen she left her home in Turin for Paris, where she studied French language and literature, before embarking on her travels to Tibet, Bali, India and Peru. Returning with a stock of wraparound skirts, or *pareos*, sandals and scarves to sell to acquaintances, Cortese, initially in partnership with her travelling companion Christophe Sauvat, developed the idea into a wholesale business. She added to the range with her own designs of specifically handcrafted textiles, and the label was launched in 1992. The first Antik Batik boutique opened in Paris in 1999.

SHISHEH OR ABHLA BHARAT EMBROIDERY

Antik Batik continues to retain an ethical, handmade approach to garment embellishment, including the technique of shisheh embroidery (**03**). The firm employs indigenous skilled hand-workers to produce haute-hippie separates, rich in detail, pattern and colour.

01. *All-over directional one-colour print (S/S 2013).*
02. *Satin-stitch embroidery with tambour beading and applied sequins (S/S 2013).*
03. *Shisheh embroidery with pearls and beads (S/S 2013).*
04. *Beadwork on a hand-crocheted base (S/S 2013).*
05. *Tambour beading and shisheh embroidery (A/W 2012).*
06. *Soutache embroidery and couched vermicelli work (S/S 2013).*
07. *All-over feather print (S/S 2013).*
08. *Handwoven Balinese-type weaving with cotton tape (S/S 2013).*
09. *All-over sequins (S/S 2013).*

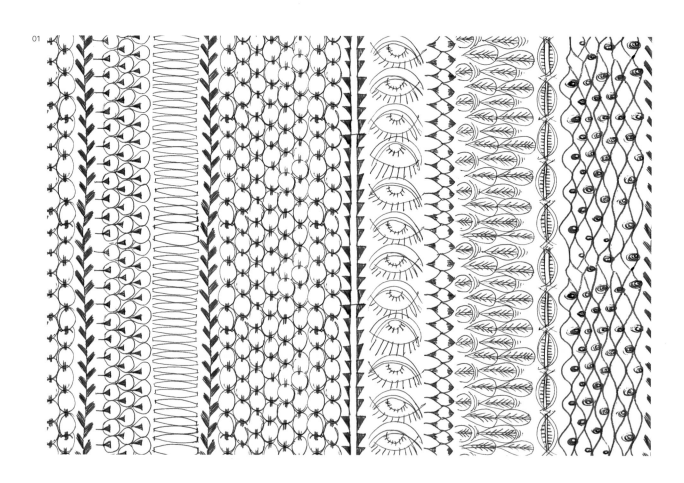

01

BARBOUR

Fulfilling the needs of sailors, fishermen and dockers, British heritage brand Barbour was established in 1894 by John Barbour and remains a family-owned business. Its outdoor clothing was popular with the military and in 1936 a range of motorcycle gear was introduced. Under the leadership of Dame Margaret Barbour, who took over in 1968, the company has a global outreach, winning the Queen's Award for Export Achievement in 1992, 1994 and 1995. Barbour has three Royal Warrants and continues to manufacture its classic wax jackets by hand in the North East of England. Collaborations have included associations with Alice Temperley and Tokihito Yoshida and a shooting clothing range with Lord James Percy.

WAXED SURFACE
Maritime oilskins evolved from the custom of proofing linen sailcloth with linseed oil in the epoch of the tea clipper. This technology was improved for clothing in the early 20th century with the use of paraffin-based waxes, which remain flexible in cold weather. The wax was applied to cotton yarn after it had been woven and dyed, and the cloth was then subjected to cupro-ammonia treatment (no longer used), which left an olive-green residual shade. The cloth was then re-waxed to reinforce the breathable weatherproof effect.

01. *Unique and distinctive 'classic' Barbour tartan.*
02. *Summer-weight dress version of the Barbour tartan (S/S 2012).*
03. *Waxed surface of the traditional Barbour all-purpose utility jacket.*

following pages
04. *The 'Daisy' parka designed for Barbour by Alice Temperley (S/S 2013).*

pages 42–3
05. *In collaboration with London store Liberty, printed linings for jackets (A/W 2008 onwards).*
06. *William Morris 'Indian' print from the Barbour Lifestyle collection (A/W 2013).*
07. *William Morris 'Golden Lily' print from the Barbour Lifestyle collection (A/W 2013).*

01

02

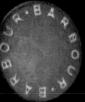

05

BASSO & BROOKE

Pioneers of digital print in fashion, the print maximalists Bruno Basso, from Brazil, and Christopher Brooke, from England, were the inaugural winners in 2004 of the Fashion Fringe Award, a competition held to search out emerging talent. The designers released their first collection under the joint label during London Fashion Week the following year, and since then their work has featured pioneering surface treatments inspired by an eclectic range of sources, from Asiatic print motifs to the work of Neo-Pop artist Jeff Koons. Basso & Brooke's innovative use of the digital printing process in a Swarovski crystal-embellished gown was recognized by the Metropolitan Museum of Art in New York when it acquired the garment in 2005. The designers continue to push the boundaries of textile technology by exploiting laser-cutting and the seamless bonding of new fabric combinations.

ENGINEERED DIGITAL PRINTING

Defined by its bold use of engineered digital prints, Basso & Brooke juxtaposes multifarious collaged images in countless permutations to produce the company's signature kaleidoscopic mix of pattern, texture and colour.

01. *'Madame Brun' digital print (A/W 2009).*
02. *'Soap Opera' digital print (A/W 2009).*
03. *'Transition' digital print (A/W 2010).*
04. *'Broken Nude' digital print (A/W 2012).*
05. *'Animale' digital print (A/W 2010).*

06. *'La Tristesse Du Roi' digital print (A/W 2012).*
07. *'Caravan' digital print (A/W 2010).*
08. *'Art Of Thrill' digital print (S/S 2012).*
09. *'Lagoon' digital print (A/W 2012).*
10. *'Stardust Variation' digital print (S/S 2011).*

following pages
11. *'Nippon Pop' digital print (S/S 2009).*
12. *'Stardust' digital print (S/S 2011).*
13. *'Sea Of Glass' digital print (A/W 2010).*
14. *'Minuet' digital print (A/W 2009).*

01
→02

04
→05

07
→08

03

06

09

11

12

13

14

16

17

18

19

TECHNIQUE

Bruno Basso is the master printmaker while Christopher Brooke strips away extraneous detail on garments to create simple silhouettes and understated clothing, such as draped dresses and softly tailored separates, as a vehicle for the prints.

previous pages
15. *'Tippi' digital print (A/W 2011).*

this page
16. *'New Flora' digital print (S/S 2009).*
17. *'Swan Lake' digital print (S/S 2010).*
18. *'Above The Clouds' digital print (S/S 2012).*
19. *'The Cult Of The One-Eyed Cat' digital print (S/S 2012).*
20. *'Exotic Fur' digital print (A/W 2010).*

BETH RICHMOND

Evoking elements of the natural world in simple graphic imagery, illustrator and textile designer Beth Richmond utilizes the craft of lino cutting to create her monochrome prints. Working across a variety of media in her London studio, the designer takes her inspiration from ethology and the anthropomorphic movement of plants, frequently travelling to Brighton and Norfolk in order to fill her sketchbooks. Fascinated with texture, Richmond uses soft linens and silks in natural duck egg blues and yellow ochres to emphasize the dramatic imprints of black crows and leaping fish. Recently commissioned to produce a large-scale lino cut for a private client, she regularly showcases her designs in exhibitions across London.

LINO CUTTING
Monochrome lino cuts make use of the material's graphic potential, exploiting bold shapes and patterns and often leaving rough-edged gouge marks in the background, as seen in swatch **02**.

01. *'Hare On Press' printed on linen (S/S 2013).*
02. *'Crow' mirrored repeat on linen (S/S 2013).*
03. *'Pilchards' printed on silk tulle (S/S 2013).*
04. *'Sardines' printed on linen (S/S 2013).*
05. *'Leaf' printed on linen (S/S 2013).*
06. *'The Bird And The Berry' printed on linen (S/S 2013).*

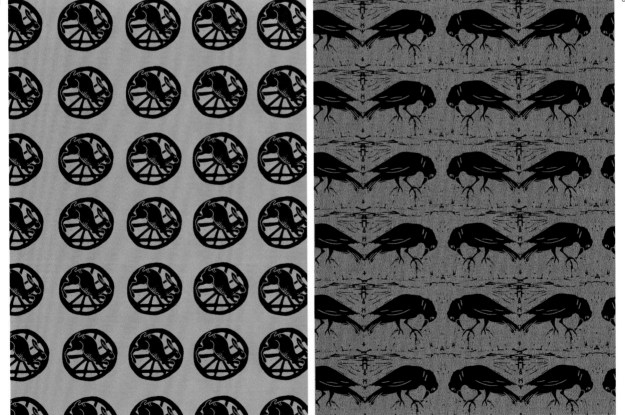

01

02

BETTY JACKSON

Understated, with an easy-to-wear ethos based on soft tailoring and an emphasis on print, Betty Jackson has been at the forefront of British fashion since the inauguration of her label in 1981. Initially employed as a freelance illustrator until 1973, Jackson worked at London label Quorum before setting up her own design company with her husband, David Cohen. In 1985 she was named British Designer of the Year; two years later she was appointed a Member of the Order of the British Empire for services to British industry and export, and she also became an elected member of the British Fashion Council. The Betty Jackson for Men collection was introduced in 1986 and the designer opened her flagship shop on Brompton Road, London, in 1991. Collaborations with British high street stores include the Autograph collection for Marks and Spencer in 2000 and she continues to design a diffusion range, Betty Jackson Black, for Debenhams. Jackson is an honorary fellow of the Royal College of Art, London, and the University of Central Lancashire, Preston.

PRINTED TEXTILES

Prints are used to add a loose opulence to cloth that is already sensual and mobile. The imagery is flowing and unhindered, reflecting the casual elegance of the style of the house. Rigid repeat is avoided, with depth and texture implied by the tonality of colour.

01. *Discharge print of poppies on a fluid silk cloth (A/W 2006).*
02. *Silk-screen print of gold foliage on silk (S/S 2002).*
03. *Abstract tree bark print in three colours on water-resistant nylon (A/W 2008).*

following pages
04. *Mosaic of faceted rectangular sequins (A/W 2008).*
05. *Three-colour stylized daisy print (S/S 2010).*

01

02

04

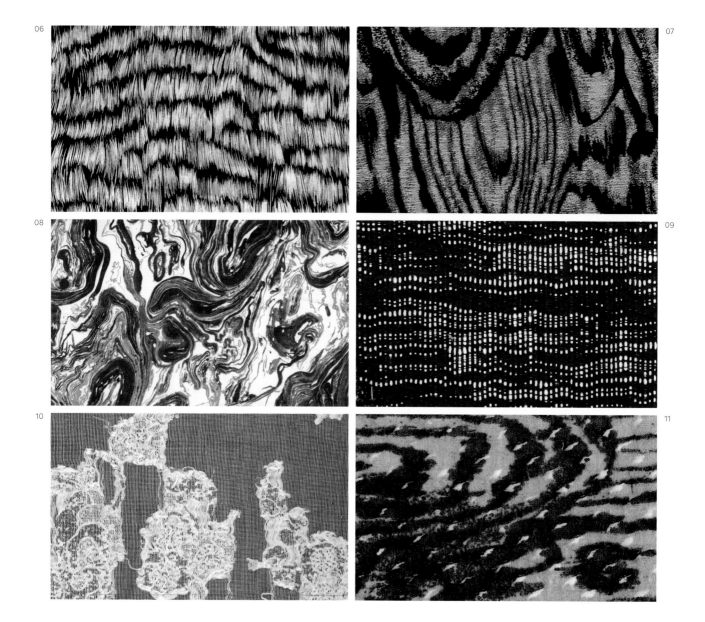

JACQUARD WEAVING

Jacquard weaving and hand embroidery are used to modulate the surfaces of a variety of materials and to evoke resonances of other textures, such as wood, pelt, marble or meadow. The aggregation of groups of texture effects across the collection adds impact to the whole from the sum of the parts.

06. *Discharge two-colour scratch print (A/W 2010).*
07. *Two-colour metallic jacquard, woodgrain print (A/W 2009).*
08. *Monochrome marble print on silk (S/S 2010).*
09. *Undulating tree bark jacquard (S/S 2011).*
10. *Chambray with loose* fil coupé *motif from secondary warp (S/S 2009).*

11. *Textured weave in wool with two-colour overprint of woodgrain (A/W 2009).*
12. *Perforated leather with raw edge silk chiffon embroidery (A/W 2002).*
13. *Leather cut-out in paisley-inspired design stitched onto mesh (S/S 2002).*

following pages
14. *Multi-colour anemone print on silk (A/W 2009).*
15. *Giant flower print on marbled monochrome ground (A/W 2008).*
16. *Scribble print on silk (S/S 2011).*

15

16

BORA AKSU

The hallmark of Turkish-born Bora Aksu is his intricate combining of contrasting layers and textures, such as softly worked chiffon juxtaposed with a structured corset base. A four-time recipient of the NEWGEN sponsorship award, the designer founded his own label immediately after graduating with a master's degree from London's Central Saint Martins College of Arts and Design in 2002. Notable collaborations include his dance costume designs for The Cathy Marston Project and work for the epic film prop designers the Artisan Armour Group. From creating demi-couture garments with highly textured surfaces to designing accessible capsule collections for ethical clothing and Fair Trade fashion label People Tree, Aksu consistently promulgates a romantic, ethereal aesthetic in a muted, subtle colour palette, utilizing handcrafted decorative elements and traditional textile craft techniques. Bora Aksu now produces four collections each year, having introduced pre-collections in 2012, as well as a hosiery line. For Autumn/Winter 2012 the label launched its first handbag collection, featuring exclusive styles, in London store Harrods.

MATCHING TONES

Ton sur ton (matching tones) variegation is achieved in a variety of materials, ranging from matt crêpe to scaly lizard skins and micro-pleated woven structures. In this way, false plains are used to interact with patterned cloth.

01. *Tonally overprinted crêpe weave (A/W 2013).*
02. *Ripple pleat on gauze ground (Pre-autumn 2013).*
03. *Reptilian leather from The Turkish Leather Co. (A/W 2013).*
04. *Shot-effect plissé weave (Pre-autumn 2013).*

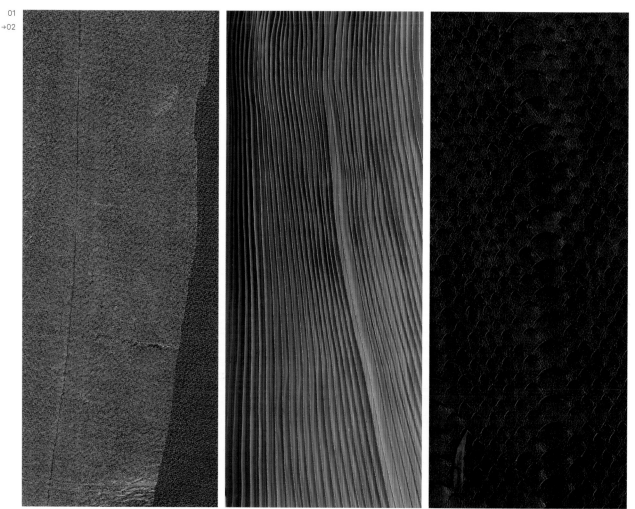

01
→02

03

LOW-CONTRAST PATTERNING

Bora Aksu uses fabrics that are characterized by low-contrast patterning, creating bespoke surfaces that have illusory or real depth of texture. Base materials are constructed using diverse technologies, from weaving to warp-knitting.

05. *Cloque jacquard brocade (A/W 2012).*
06. *Devoré satin (S/S 2013).*
07. *Cut brocade applied to tulle with satin stitch (S/S 2010).*
08. *Tonal print on chiffon (S/S 2013).*
09. *Raschel knit with overlaid threads (A/W 2013).*
10. *Raschel warp-knit with bouclé overlay (A/W 2013).*
11. *Overprinted raschel warp-knit lace (S/S 2013).*

BRUCE OLDFIELD

Bruce Oldfield founded his own ready-to-wear company in 1975, two years after graduating from Central Saint Martins College of Arts and Design, London. The label initially specialized in premium market occasion clothing but had moved into couture by 1983, offering exclusive glamorous styles to private clients. The company maintained both ready-to-wear and couture lines from 1984 and its enviable client list ranged from Hollywood stars to royalty, including Diana, Princess of Wales. Oldfield has been honoured both within the fashion industry and in the wider community.

TECHNIQUE

The red carpet and special occasion market has a particular appetite for silk; it is the fibre of choice for demonstrative embellishment. The craft of hand embroidery offers unlimited patterning possibility that is often used in tonal colour as a false plain.

01. *Three-dimensional flower in sequins on an overlapping sequin ground (Spring 2013).*
02. *Appliquéd individual organza leaves , bugle beads and sequins (Winter 2012).*
03. *Art burnished sequin zig-zag design (A/W 2012).*
04. *Tone-on-tone three-dimensional flowers appliquéd on an overlapping sequin ground (Spring 2013).*
05. *Machine-embroidered ribbon on organza by Italian company Ruffo Coli (S/S 2012).*

following pages
06. *Re-embroidered lace by French company Solstiss (c. 1995).*
07. *Machine-made guipure lace by Italian company Marco Lagattolla (2009).*
08. *Re-embroidered lace by French company Jean Bracq (1995).*
09. *Metallic lace by Jean Bracq.*
10. *Guipure lace by Swiss company Forster Rohner (2012).*

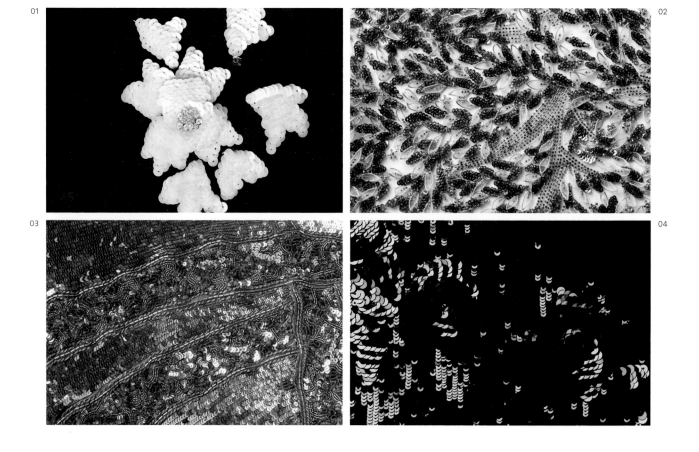

01

02

03

04

06

11. *Hand-embroidered 'shadow work' hydrangea blooms on silk georgette (S/S 2013).*

12. *Wedding dress commission; rose embroidery on silk organza using gold bullion, bugle beads and sequins (2013).*

13. *Rambling rose finely traced in dull gold bullion, organza on silk tulle (S/S 2013).*

14. *Wedding dress commission for Lady Percy; organza leaf appliqués on a floral framework in bugle beads (Summer 2013).*

15. *Wedding dress sample; laser-cut silk flowers, cloth covered beads and a tracery of silver-cut beads (Spring 2011).*

TECHNIQUE

The impact of cloth can be enhanced greatly by creating variegation in the surface, either through engineering structural differentiation in the assemblages of yarn or through modifying the constructed surface with additional finishing effects.

16. *Engineered tears on a delicate silk chiffon by Canepa, overprinted with irregular spots (S/S 2010).*

17. *Blistered lacquer-effect silk and viscose jacquard by Mantero (A/W 2013).*

18. *1970s-inspired silk geometric jacquard (A/W 2011).*

19. *Silk and Lurex blister jaquard by Ruffo Coli (S/S 2011).*

20. *Silk and wool jacquard by Carlo Pozzi (A/W 2012).*

21. *Black silk jacquard overprinted in gold by Mantero (A/W 2013).*

22. *'Vorticist' silk and wool jacquard by Mantero (A/W 2013).*

CARLO VOLPI

Italian-born Carlo Volpi elevates the traditional craft of hand-knitting to high fashion with an imaginative and playful exploration of scale and texture. London-based since 1998, Volpi graduated from the Royal College of Art in 2012. Since then, he has worked as a freelance designer of men's knitwear and on commissions. He has also taught in a number of UK colleges and regularly works on projects for the research area at the Pitti Filati trade show in Florence. The designer has been the recipient of several awards, including the Worshipful Company of Haberdashers' Award and the Worshipful Company of Framework Knitters' Award. Volpi is also a freelance writer for knittingindustry.com and he collaborates on the knitwear forecast for *Textile View* magazine.

BOHUS HAND-KNITTING

Bohus hand-knitting, a stranded colour knitting technique similar to that of intarsia and Fair Isle knitting, is deployed by Volpi in swatches **08** and **13**. Bohus knitting takes its name from an organization in Sweden called Bohus Stickning.

01. *Swatch knitted on a 12gg Shima Seiki in cashwool (May 2012).*

02. *Jacquard knitted on a chunky domestic machine in wool (November 2011).*

03. *Plaited rib knitted in lambswool on a 5gg Dubied machine (October 2011).*

04. *Jacquard knitted in lambswool on a standard gauge domestic machine (May 2010).*

following pages

05. *Brioche hand-knitting in wool (May 2010).*

06. *Swatch knitted in cotton on a 12gg Dubied machine (May 2010).*

07. *Two-colour brioche rib knitted on a 12gg Shima Seiki (May 2012).*

08. *A combination of slip stitch and Bohus hand-knit in linen/ cotton (March 2013).*

09. *Plaited check knitted in a lambswool angora mix on a standard gauge domestic machine (May 2010).*

10. *Stripes with embroidery and woven details in wool (November 2011).*

11. *Brioche hand-knitted cables and fringes in wool/mohair knitted on a standard gauge domestic machine (June 2012).*

12. *Woollen jacquard with pintucks (July 2012).*

13. *Combination of slip stitch and Bohus hand-knit in wool (March 2013).*

14. *Stripes with embroidery and needle weaving (November 2011).*

01
→02

03

04

05
→06

07

08
→09

10

11
→12

13

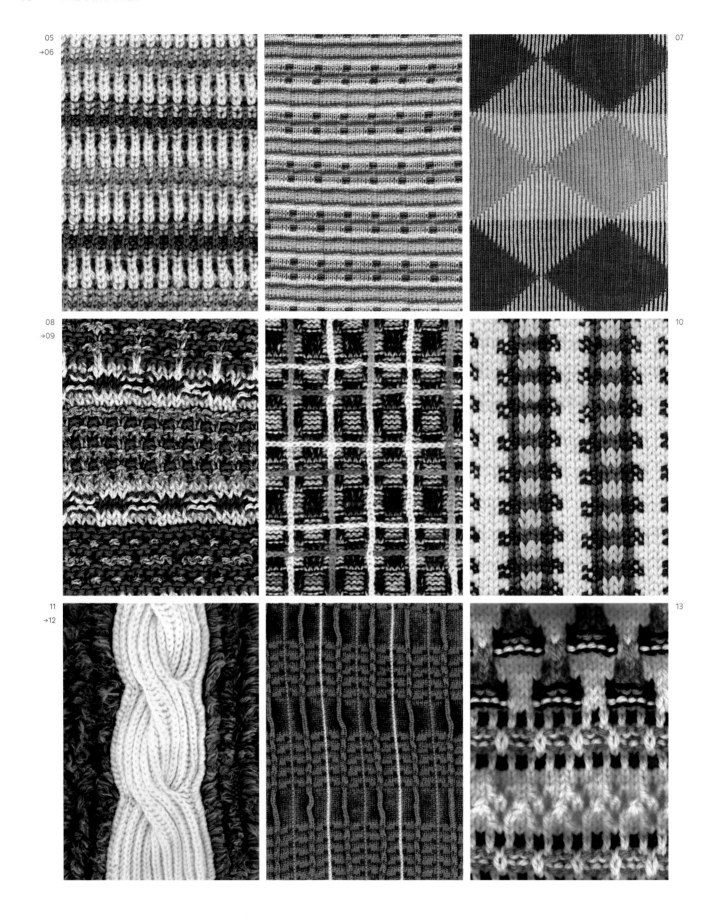

15

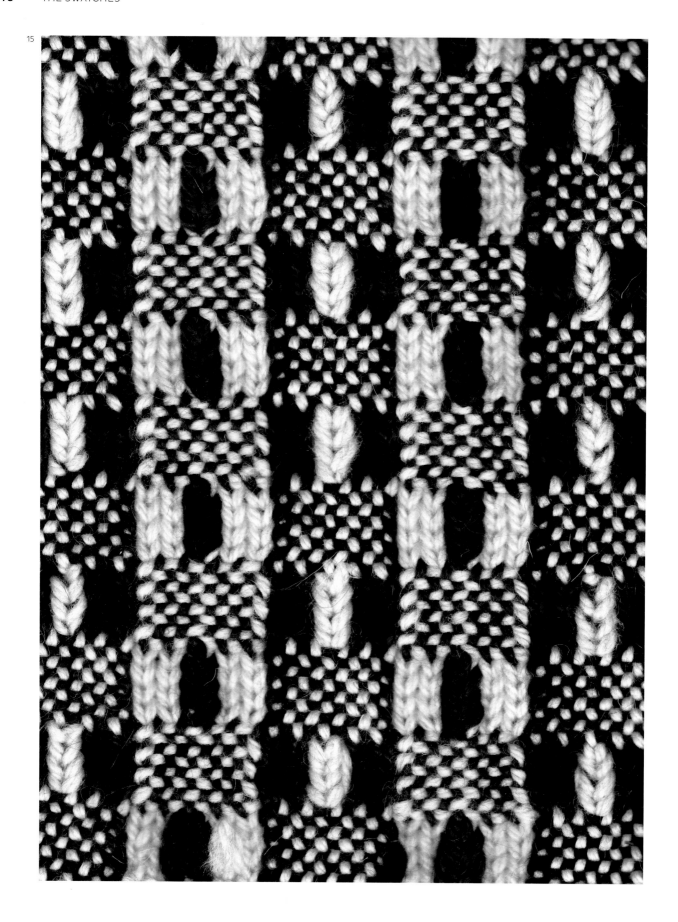

15. *Stripes with embroidery and needle weaving (November 2011).*

16. *Stripes with embroidery and needle weaving (November 2011).*

17. *Jacquard knitted in wool/mohair on a domestic machine (January 2012).*

18. *Hand embroidery on cashwool (July 2012).*

19. *Checks with embroidery (November 2011).*

following pages

20. *Swatch knitted in cotton on a 12gg Dubied machine (April 2010).*

21. *Reverse of jacquard knitted on a domestic machine (January 2013).*

20

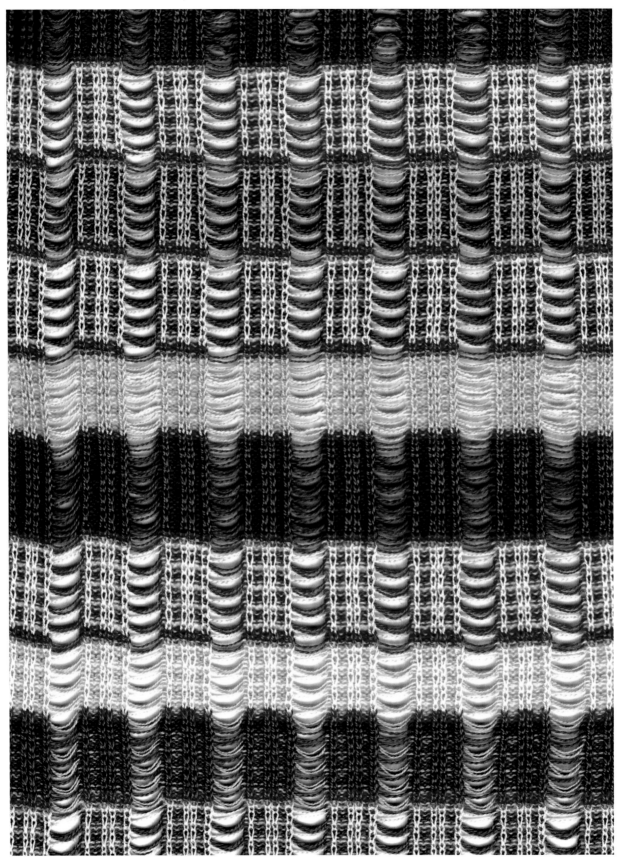

CHARLOTTE TAYLOR

With her distinctive graphic style comprising a rigid array of motifs in signature two-colour prints, British-born Charlotte Taylor developed her eponymous womenswear label in 2009. This was launched to great acclaim at London Fashion Week in February 2010. After graduating from Central Saint Martins College of Arts and Design, London, Taylor worked in the creative marketing department of fashion designer Luella Bartley, gaining valuable experience.

SCREEN-PRINTING
Taylor utilizes the screen-printing process for her bold graphic statements. The quirky and idiosyncratic motifs are printed in the length and set in simple half-drop repeats (**01**) or mirrored drop repeats (**05**).

01. *Two-colour screen print, creating a 'powdered' effect (A/W 2011).*
02. *Two-colour screen print (A/W 2011).*

A diffusion line, Charlotte by Charlotte Taylor, was put on the market in September 2011 in conjunction with American retailer Anthropologie, which has stores across the USA and the UK. Variations of scale and colour of the print designs are fashioned into simple understated garments featuring soft tailoring: jackets, gently gathered knee-length skirts, demure high-buttoning blouses and free-flowing maxidresses.

03. *A two-colour screen print (A/W 2011).*
04. *A two-colour screen print with a directional bias effect (S/S 2012).*
05. *A two-colour screen print (S/S 2012).*
06. *A two-colour screen print, exploiting radial symmetry (S/S 2012).*
07. *A two-colour screen print (S/S 2012).*
08. *A two-colour screen print, creating a striped parade (A/W 2011 and S/S 2013).*

01
→02

03

04
→05

06

07

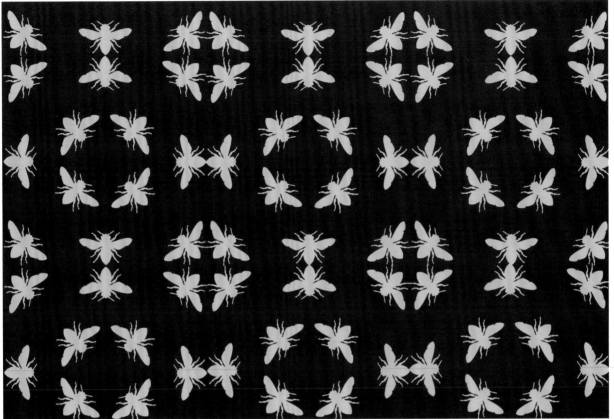

08

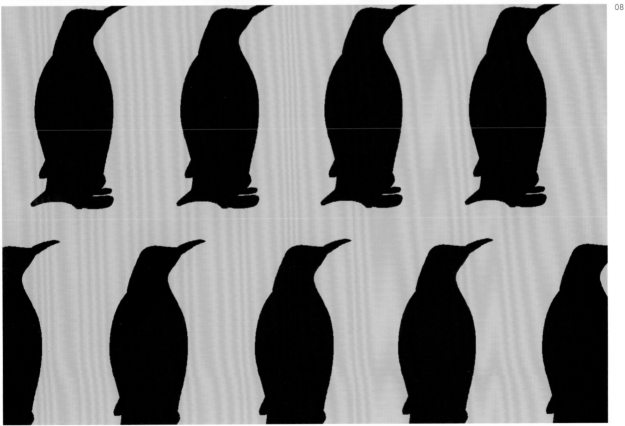

CHRISTOPHER KANE

Born in a former mining village in Scotland, Christopher Kane established a global brand with the backing of powerful luxury goods conglomerate PPR (Pinault-Printemps-Redoute, subsequently Kering), which bought 51 per cent of the business in 2013. The designer's graduate collection led to the offer of a full-time job from Donatella Versace, which he refused, later agreeing to work as a consultant and designer for the Versace ready-to-wear line Versus. Kane showed his first collection of neon body-conscious dresses under his own name in 2006 to international acclaim. Working with Tammy Kane, his sister, business partner and creative collaborator, the designer has collected a number of awards, including New Designer of the Year at the British Fashion Awards in 2007.

HEAT-SEALED APPLIQUÉ
Cut-out flowers are carefully positioned and floated between layers of 70 per cent aluminium organza, creating an optical illusion as seen in swatches **06** and **07**.

01. *Rhinestone-encrusted latticework (S/S 2012).*
02. *Embellished denim in collaboration with J Brand (S/S 2012).*
03. *Embellished denim in collaboration with J Brand (S/S 2012).*
04. *Rhinestone-encrusted latticework (S/S 2012).*
05. *Two layers of cut lace on a woven lamé background (Resort 2012).*

following pages
06. *Cut-out flowers appliquéd beneath layers of organza (S/S 2012).*
07. *Cut-out flowers appliquéd beneath layers of organza (S/S 2012).*

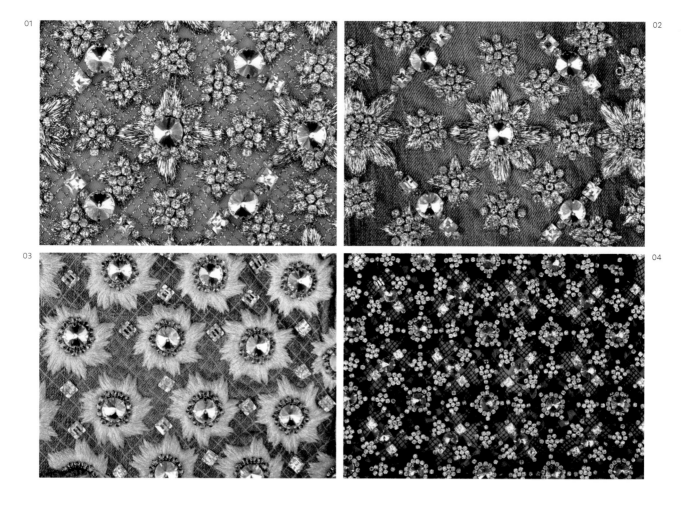

01

02

03

04

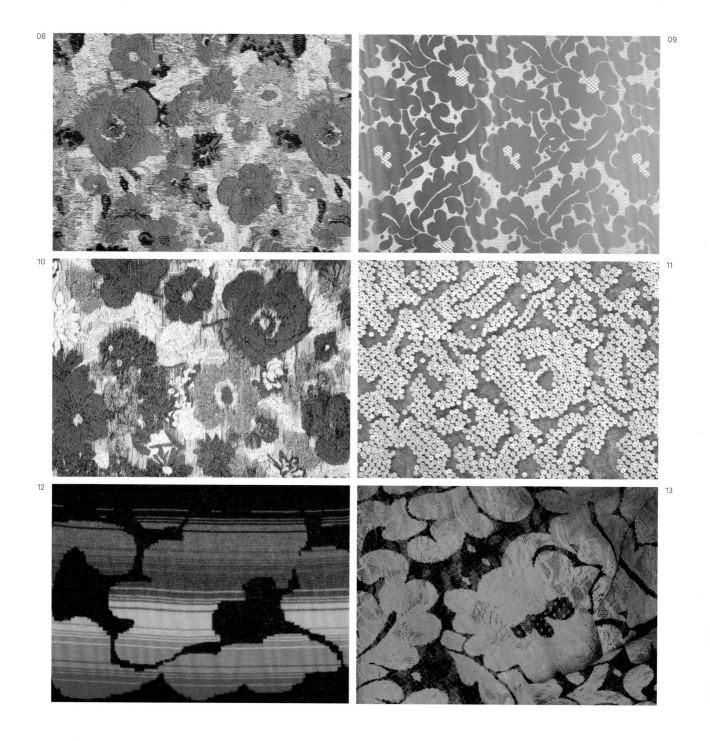

BROCADE

The richly figured surface of the silk brocade seen in swatches **01**, **03** and **04** is the result of a supplementary weft, creating the impression of an embroidered fabric. It is matched in scale to the floral motif of the lace.

08. *Jacquard floral figured brocade (S/S 2012).*
09. *All-over neon Leavers lace (Resort 2012).*
10. *Jacquard lamé brocade (S/S 2012).*
11. *Sequins on a tulle net base (S/S 2012).*
12. *Ladder-back jacquard sweater in space-dyed yarn (Resort 2012).*
13. *Close-up of Leavers lace (S/S 2012).*
14. *Polychromatic striped all-over Leavers lace (Resort 2012).*

CLUNY LACE*

The single remaining manufacturer of Leavers lace in the UK, Cluny Lace produces a wide range of products for leading international designers and couturiers, including Vivienne Westwood, Oscar de la Renta and Dolce & Gabbana. Situated at the heart of Britain's textile industry on the Nottinghamshire and Derbyshire borders, the purpose-designed factory was built at the beginning of the 20th century to hold the specialized lace machines. The company is owned and managed by the eighth and ninth generations of the Mason family, who began manufacturing lace in the 1760s at the start of Britain's Industrial Revolution. Since that time, Cluny Lace has continued to build up a portfolio of hundreds of lace patterns, all of which are unique to the company. Many of the designs were drafted by Frank Maltby Mason and Francis Bowler Mason, the sixth and seventh generations of the family.

LEAVERS LACE

Leavers lace is made by a machine that replicates handmade lace by twisting the threads together on giant ten-tonne frames designed in 1814. The process is employed by the company to manufacture Cluny all-over lace designs, edgings and insertions, as well as Leavers fine cotton, Valenciennes-style lace all-overs, edgings, galloons and insertions.

01. *Elements of the edging lace were cut out and appliquéd to the train of the wedding dress worn by Catherine Middleton, now the Duchess of Cambridge. These were then expertly crafted into place by seamstresses at the Royal School of Needlework in London.*

02. *Narrow edging lace adorned the underskirt to the wedding dress worn by Catherine Middleton. Cluny Lace also supplied the edging laces that adorned the dresses of the bridesmaids.*

following pages
03. *From the Cluny lace sample book, varieties of edging lace, insertions and galloons.*
04. *White cotton edging lace for Oscar de la Renta (S/S 2012 and 2013).*

01

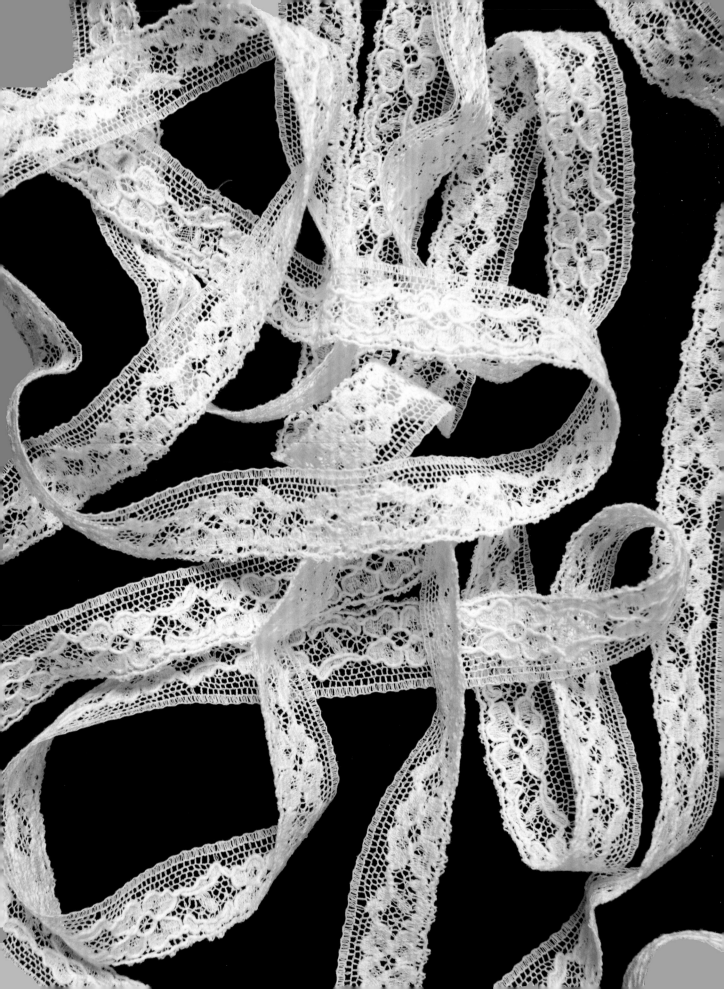

03

CLUNY LACE FOR VIVIENNE WESTWOOD

05. *All-over Cluny lace for Vivienne Westwood Gold label (S/S 2012).*

CLUNY LACE FOR JEAN PAUL GAULTIER

06. *Narrow Cluny lace for Jean Paul Gaultier (S/S 2007).*

CLUNY LACE FOR VIVIENNE WESTWOOD

07. *All-over Cluny lace for Vivienne Westwood Gold label (S/S 2012).*

08

09

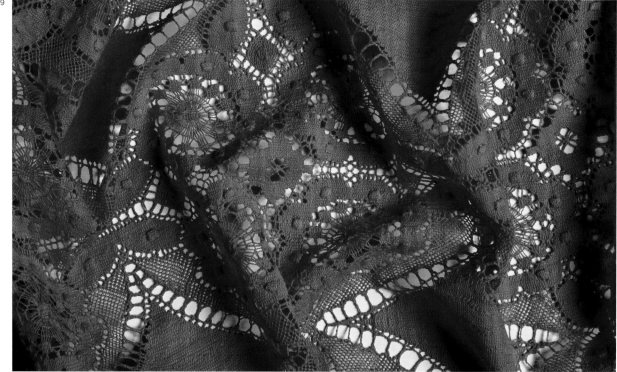

CLUNY LACE FOR ROBERTO CAVALLI

08. *Cluny cotton insertion lace for Roberto Cavalli (S/S 2008).*

CLUNY LACE FOR DOLCE & GABBANA

09–10. *All-over designs in cotton Cluny lace produced in several colours for Dolce & Gabbana (RTW S/S 2010).*

THE COLORFIELD

With the premise that colour is the key to a successful print collection, The Colorfield defines a directional colour palette at the start of each season. The company was launched in New York City in 1994 by Adam Read, and his business partner, Paul Harding, joined a few years later as the enterprise expanded. Named after the 1960s US art movement that focused on colour, the studio quickly became an established presence at major print shows in the USA and Europe. In 2005 The Colorfield expanded by opening a studio in London's Bermondsey area, and it now houses a full design team comprising fifteen artists/designers. The New York studio is mainly a showroom and sales base from which the collection is sold throughout the USA, Europe and the Far East by a dedicated sales team.

'WET' AND DIGITAL MEDIA

Although computer-aided design and the ability to print directly from digital media have evolved to sophisticated levels over the last thirty years, in many respects the visual results and terminology remain faithful to the hand techniques of the traditional studio. All software packages for the manipulation of imagery, such as Photoshop, incorporate menus of filters and effects that owe their source – and names – to the heritage of the creative studio. It is not uncommon for specialist studios to mix 'wet' and digital media in the development of final design work, harnessing the sensitivity of handwork to the productivity of digital processes.

01. *Offset geometric print for White House Black Market (July 2012).*
02. *Swirling impressionistic print in monochrome for Bon-Ton (February 2011).*
03. *Chevron mosaic print for Belk department stores (July 2012).*
04. *Aboriginal painting-style leopard-skin print for Femteks (September 2011).*
05. *Grassy undergrowth print on dark ground for McSchreiber (September 2011).*

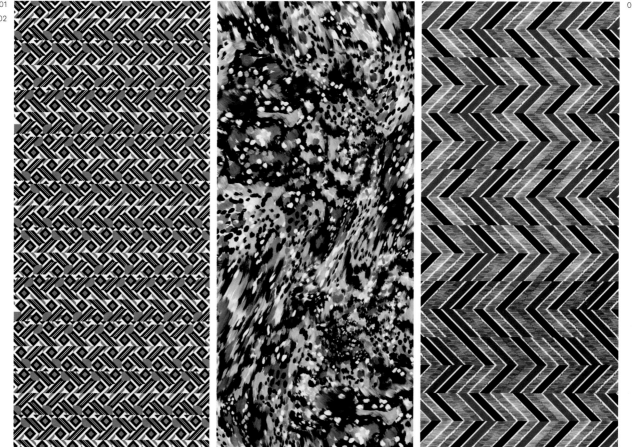

01
→02

03

04

05

06
→07

08

09
→10

11

12
→13

14

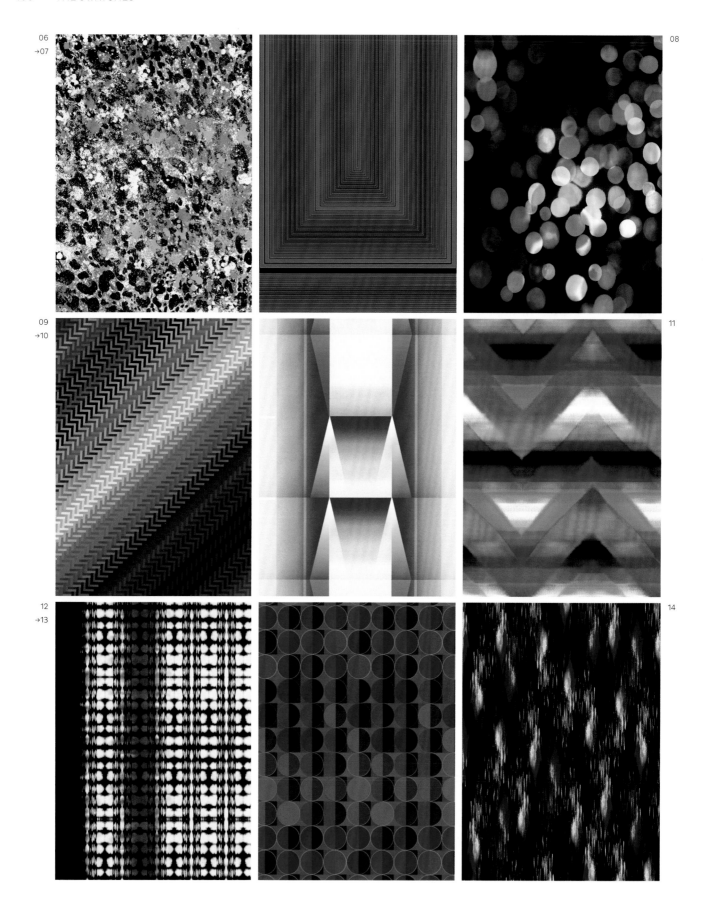

16

17

previous pages

06. *Technicolour sprayed leopard print for Olsen (February 2011).*

07. *All-over geometric print on crêpe de Chine for Trina Turk (October 2012).*

08. *City lights nocturnal print for Ports 1961 (July 2012).*

09. *Herringbone spectrum stripe print for Trina Turk (October 2012).*

10. *Angular Art Deco print for Ports 1961 (January 2012).*

11. *Bright Art Deco chevron print for Macy's Style & Co. (December 2010).*

12. *Graphic grid print for Vince Camuto (July 2012).*

13. *Tonal dot grid print for Kohl's (September 2011).*

14. *Streaky diamond texture print for Ports 1961 (July 2012).*

15. *Angular geometric print for fabric converter John Kaldor (November 2011).*

this page

16. *Banded baroque tonal print for Jones NY (September 2011).*

17. *Striated lotus print for Tillsonburg Apparel, Hong Kong (September 2011).*

18. *Primitive monochrome geometric print for Belford (September 2011).*

19. *Micro geometric print for Calvin Klein (August 2012).*

20. *Shibori-inspired print for Soul Star Clothing (August 2012).*

21. *Kaleidoscopic floral print for Belk department stores (July 2012).*

22. *Layered baroque print with woven textures for Soma (September 2011).*

23. *Tinted snakeskin print for Karen Millen (November 2011).*

24

this page
24. Fragmented bias grid print for Ellen Tracy (March 2011).
25. Print of scalloped, pleated fringing for Guarisco Class (February 2011).

following pages
26. Detailed layered floral garland for Victoria's Secret (September 2011).
27. All-over floral print in the style of chintz for Victoria's Secret (September 2011).
28. Pop art poppy print for Olivier Strelli (February 2011).

29. Delicate botanical print for Banana Republic (September 2011).
30. Dense painterly floral print for J Crew (March 2011).
31. Art Deco-influenced floral print for Lane Bryant womenswear (July 2012).
32. Dense graphic floral for Dana Buchman swimwear (September 2011).
33. Floral print in graded washes for Ports 1961 (October 2012).
34. Anemones print for Lane Bryant (July 2012).
35. Floral study in graded washes on solid ground for Fat Face. (February 2011).

26
→27

28

29
→30

31

32
→33

34

THE COLOUR UNION

Creating bespoke, quirky, theatrical, iconic and opulent textiles, Zara Siddiqui-Lester is the owner and designer of The Colour Union, a label that reflects her passionate engagement with colour. Siddiqui-Lester is an established textile designer who produces commissions for a diverse client base that includes Liberty and the National Gallery in London and Bloomingdale's in New York. She has also worked as a course director at the University of the Arts London, specializing in creative entrepreneurship, colour psychology, and fashion and textile trends.

DIGITAL PRINTING

Digital printing techniques enable a vast number of images to be reproduced simply, in one stage, while achieving great depth of colour.

01. *'HRH', commissioned by Royal Mail. Each stamp was scanned and set into a grid to form a multicoloured sheet of stamps. Colour management was crucial as the finished printed stamps needed to be as close as possible to the originals. Each stamp has a solid background colour with the image a tone of that colour. This cotton velvet fabric was one of many stamp combinations used for a variety of products (2010).*

02–03. *Sections taken from 'Picture Perfect Patchwork', a visual history of designs created by combining various designs by The Colour Union with Old Master portraits from copyright-free image libraries. Each image is set into a grid using Photoshop and enhanced for greater clarity when digitally printed onto cotton velvet, which has a pile. The definition is achieved by a final design at 300dpi (dots per inch) (2013).*

01

02

03

DASH AND MILLER

Launched by designers Juliet Bailey and Franki Brewer in 2009, Bristol-based company Dash and Miller offers a bespoke, handwoven design service to the fashion and interior industries in Europe, the USA, China and Japan. The company specializes in the design, development and production of woven fabrics and also collaborates with a high-end UK womenswear mill to produce seasonal collections of fabric available by the metre. Franki Brewer's previous experience includes working with several London-based handwoven textile design studios, and she has also designed for one of the UK's most highly acclaimed bespoke interior design companies. Juliet Bailey gained experience in innovative textile manufacture for womenswear and interiors in Switzerland and industrial design development for interiors in the Far East, and has done extensive freelance design work for woven and printed textiles in the UK.

DOBBY WEAVING

The constraint inherent in dobby weaving places the onus on the designer to create an interplay of structure with colour in warp and weft that optimizes the impact of the yarn and cloth.

01. *Handwoven design; dobby block threading; silk warp with wool and Lurex weft (July 2012).*
02. *Handwoven design; dobby extra-weft pattern; silk warp with silk and Lurex weft (September 2010).*
03. *Handwoven design; dobby distorted weft technique; silk warp with silk and cotton chenille weft (May 2012).*
04. *Handwoven design; dobby geometric twill pattern; silk warp and weft (April 2013).*
05. *Handwoven design; dobby block geometric pattern; silk warp and weft (January 2013).*
06. *Handwoven design; dobby block geometric pattern with stripe ground; silk warp with silk, Lurex and neon polyester weft (January 2013).*
07. *Handwoven design; dobby extra-weft geometric distorted pattern; cotton warp with silk weft (April 2012).*

01

02

03

04

05

06

07

this page

08. *Handwoven design; dobby extra-weft herringbone with
block twill ground; silk warp with silk and wool blend weft
(April 2013).*

09. *Handwoven design; dobby block geometric pattern with
fancy tweed ground; silk warp with silk, wool, Lurex and
polyurethane coated weft (July 2012).*

10. *Handwoven design; dobby extra-weft novelty pattern;
cotton warp with wool weft (April 2012).*

11. *Handwoven design; dobby fancy warp and weft tweed;
cotton, cotton chenille, polyurethane coated and sequin
yarn, warp and weft (February 2013).*

12. *Jacquard woven fabric for Barbara Tfank; distorted weft
in check pattern; silk warp with neon polyester and cotton
weft (Spring 2013).*

following pages

13. *Handwoven design; dobby geometric ombré pattern;
silk warp and weft (April 2013).*

DASHING TWEEDS*

Founded by Scottish-born woven textile designer Kirsty McDougall and photographer Guy Hills in 2006, Dashing Tweeds combines the heritage of tweed and the use of technical yarn to produce bespoke fabrics that not only have a sense of tradition but also promote innovation and function. The textile brand is committed to working in collaboration with British mills, and all production is carried out within the UK. Following McDougall's graduation from the Royal College of Art in London in 2002, the Victoria and Albert Museum acquired two examples of her woven, printed and embroidered textiles for its permanent collection of European textiles. Dashing Tweeds's development of a reflective tweed suiting – 'lumatwill' – led to a small collection of menswear being designed and stocked internationally. Through her studio, McDougall also designs and develops woven multimedia textiles for many major fashion houses, in the UK and internationally, and has collaborated with the film and science sectors.

TWEED STRUCTURES

Fine reflective filaments are woven into woollen suiting using a variety of new and traditional structures that allude to the tweed aesthetic. Designs are based around traditional checks, twills and herringbones, and colour inspiration comes from the changing surrounding environment.

01. *'Shetland Jig'. Shetland wool satin and sateen block weave (2011).*
02. *'The Dashing Explorer Harris Tweed'. A 2/2 twill (2010).*
03. *Black and charcoal merino wool with basket-effect colour and weave. A 2/2 twill (2010).*
04. *Multi-colour merino wool. A 2/2 twill check with reflective yarn (2008).*
05. *'New Wave'. A multi-colour merino wool undulating twill with ombré warp and weft (2008).*
06. *A merino satin and satin block weave (2009).*

07. *'Green Raver'. A merino and reflective yarn undulating twill with an ombré warp (2009).*
08. *'The Beagler'. A merino and reflective broken twill check (2007).*
09. *A merino Prince of Wales check. A 4/4 twill (2010).*
10. *'The Sketcher'. A silk, linen and wool summer herringbone with striped warp (2012).*

following pages
11. *'Special Modernist'. A merino twill derivative diamond weave with an ombré warp. (2011)*
12. *'The Dashing Stripe'. A merino wool, satin and twill stripe. (2009)*
13. *'Turquoise Peak'. A merino chevron weave. (2010)*
14. *'Hyde Park Check'. A merino Prince of Wales check with a 2/2 twill. (2011)*

01

02

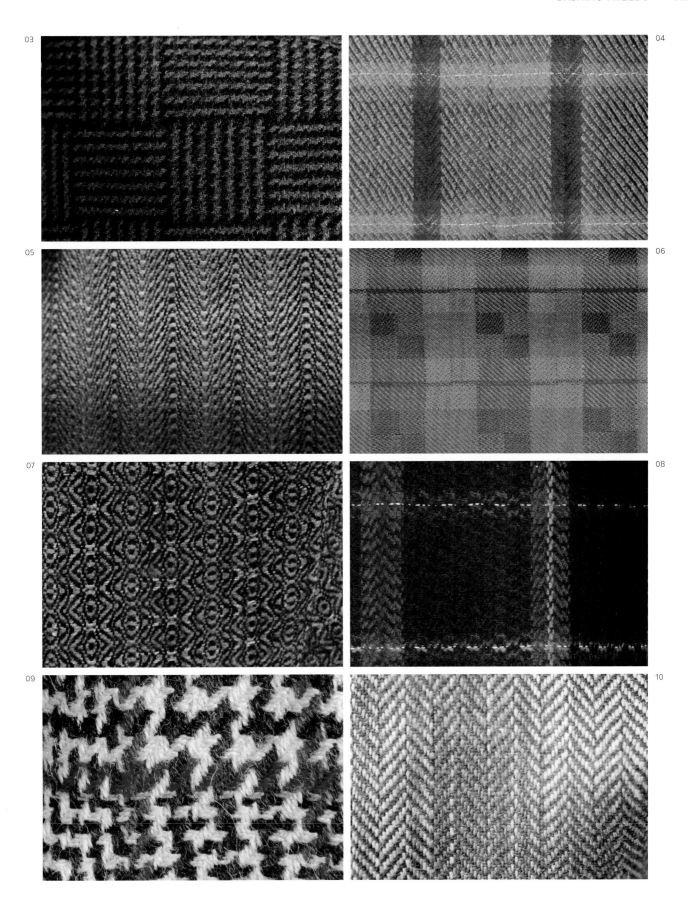

11

12

13

14

DAVID KOMA

Born in Georgia but now based in London, fashion innovator David Koma (David Komakhidze) embellishes a sculptural and controlled silhouette with intricate, experimental techniques such as laser-cutting. The designer studied at London's Central Saint Martins College of Arts and Design, and his final undergraduate collection won their Best Womenswear Award in 2007. He graduated from the MA fashion course with distinction in 2009 and he was awarded the Harrods Design Award for the industrial, architectural and sci-fi-inspired designs of his collection of body-conscious dresses. More recently Koma designed a five-piece line for British high street store Topshop, and he also received NEWGEN catwalk sponsorship to show at London Fashion Week in February 2012. His work is inspired by André Courrèges, Pierre Cardin and Thierry Mugler, among others.

LASER-CUTTING

Koma uses laser-cutting to perforate the surface of the upper layer of the garment with variously scaled polka dots, inspired by the work of Japanese artist Yayoi Kusama. These are then laid over ombréd coloured circles, creating a playful juxtaposition of scale and colour.

THREE-DIMENSIONAL BEADING

Koma collaborated with jewelry designer Sarah Angold to create three-dimensional Perspex pieces to highlight details of dresses at the neck and hem. The shards of transparent plastic are hinged at the base to create movement.

01. *High spectrum Donegal tweed with knickerbocker yarn (A/W 2012).*
02. *Laser-cut felt laminated with leather (A/W 2011).*
03. *Laser-cut felted wool superimposed on printed satin with fur pom-poms (A/W 2012).*

following pages
04. *Three-dimensional beading in collaboration with Sarah Angold (S/S 2012).*

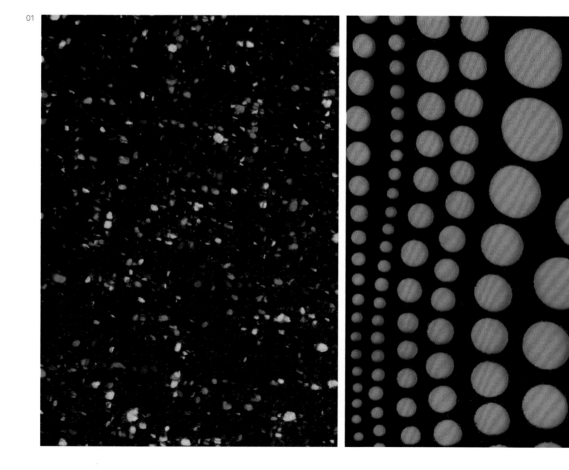

01

02

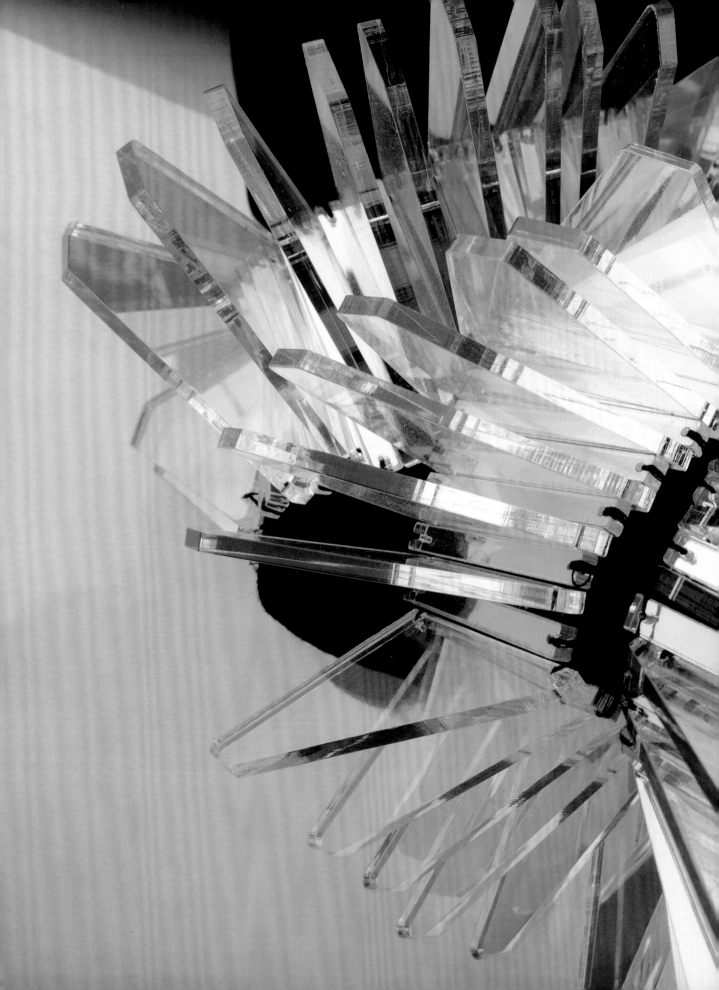

DAY BIRGER ET MIKKELSEN

One of the first of the Danish brands to make its mark on the international fashion scene, Day Birger et Mikkelsen, conflates traditional craft processes with vintage-inspired glamour. Launched in 1997, the label is known for its bohemian approach to Scandinavian simplicity, prompted by the global travels of founder and owner Keld Mikkelsen. His aesthetic of delicately detailed dresses and embellished pieces is tempered by elements of masculine tailoring. The visual identity of the label has also extended into a homeware range, with Mikkelsen's wife, Marianne Brandi, as the head designer of the interior design line Day Home, introduced in 2005. Their daughter, Amalie, is the inspiration behind 2nd Day, a younger diffusion line launched in 2011.

DISCHARGE PRINTING

The technique of discharge printing (also known as extract printing) is used to create a lighter pattern on a dark ground, seen in swatch **05**, forming a subtle yet intricate motif in keeping with the label's design ethos.

01. *Vermicelli tambour beading on georgette (S/S 2012).*
02. *Micro sequins stitched to jersey (S/S 2012).*
03. *Burnished pintucked leather (S/S 2012).*
04. *Venetian* point de neige *needlepoint lace (S/S 2012).*
05. *Baroque paisley printed cartouche (S/S 2012).*
06. *Discharge print on finished garment (S/S 2012).*

DIOR

RAF SIMONS AT DIOR

In 2012 Christian Dior invited Belgian-born designer Raf Simons to take over the most coveted role in fashion: creative head of Dior. Since his appointment, Simons has displayed an understanding of the house's legacy, subtly reshaping Dior's classic lines alongside his own inimitable handwriting. With a background that includes a degree in industrial and furniture design and an internship with fellow

Belgian designer Walter Van Beirendonck in 1990, Simons showed his first menswear collection in Milan in 1995. After a period as head of the fashion department at the University of Applied Arts in Vienna, he was named creative director of menswear and womenswear for arch minimalist label Jil Sander in 2005. The designer presented his first couture collection for the House of Dior in 2012.

HAND EMBROIDERY

The affinity of hand embroidery with couture production lies in its ability to confect opulent embellishment to the precise garment form. This is often attained by preparing shaped overlays of flimsy tulle or voile, loaded with pattern in beads, crystals, silk flowers or threads, which are then superimposed onto a more substantial background fabric. Dedicated to hand embroidery, the atelier Maison Vermont has serviced the couture industry since 1956 and was acquired by Dior in 2012.

01. *Handcrafted arched constructions of sequins, beads and crystals, mounted on silk tulle (RTW S/S 2013).*

02. *Three-dimensional hand embroidery, engineered organically to the form of the garment (RTW A/W 2013).*

following pages

03. *A spidery filigree of sequin ribbons stitched to diaphanous silk tulle (Haute Couture S/S 2013).*

04. *Simple wild flowers in cut fabric, beads and threads of chain stitch on tulle (Haute Couture S/S 2013).*

05. *Exotic feathers form embroidered flowers on an opaque twill ground (Haute Couture A/W 2013).*

06. *A swathe of nocturnal blossom crafted in shaped and simple beads (Haute Couture S/S 2013).*

07. *Ethereal discharge print on silk organza (Cruise 2014).*

01

03

04

05

06

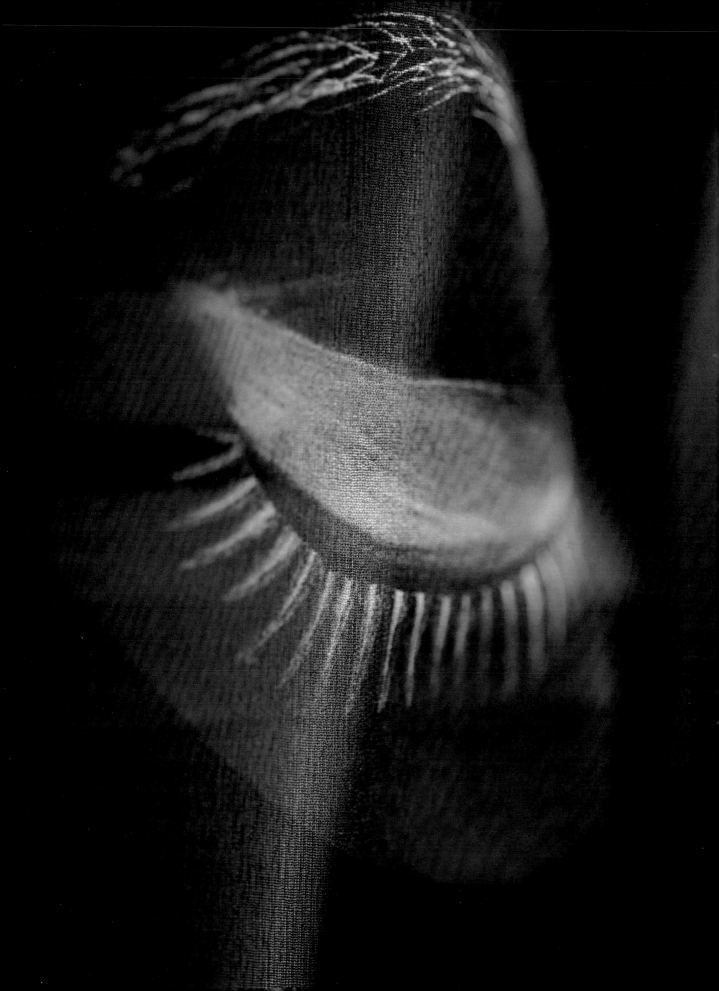

ELEY KISHIMOTO

The Eley Kishimoto label is one of the most enduring and recognizable of London's creative brands. Its two principals, Mark Eley and Wakako Kishimoto, have described themselves as 'surface decorators'; patterned and decorative textiles boasting vibrant, playful motifs are central to their approach. The duo established themselves in 1992 working as consultants for companies including Louis Vuitton, Marc Jacobs, Alexander McQueen, Alber Elbaz and Jil Sander, before launching their own label in 1996. Cross-branding design collaborations include motorcycle helmets for Ateliers Ruby, jewelry for Vendome, Ben Wilson chairs, G-Wiz electric cars and a range for Italian sportswear brand Ellesse.

SCREEN-PRINTED TEXTILES
Rooted in a design philosophy that reveres the handcrafted process, Eley Kishimoto's bold graphics are balanced with demure and idiosyncratic garment styling. The 'Flash' print (**09**) has become something of a modern classic.

01. *'Tricky Sleeves' (A/W 2008).*
02. *'Spinning Man' (S/S 2005).*

following pages
03. *'Ba Ba Bloom' (S/S 2009).*
04. *'Feathers' (S/S 2010).*
05. *'Birdy Sky' (S/S 2002).*
06. *'Ropey' (S/S 2002).*
07. *'Horses' (A/W 2008).*
08. *'Landscape' (A/W 2001).*
09. *'Flash' (S/S 2001).*

01

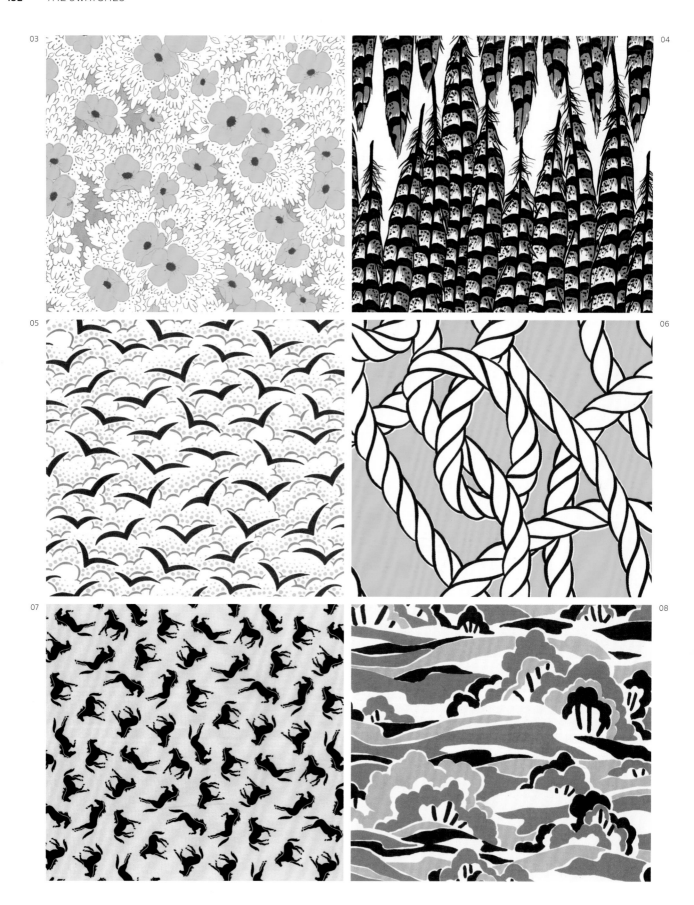

10

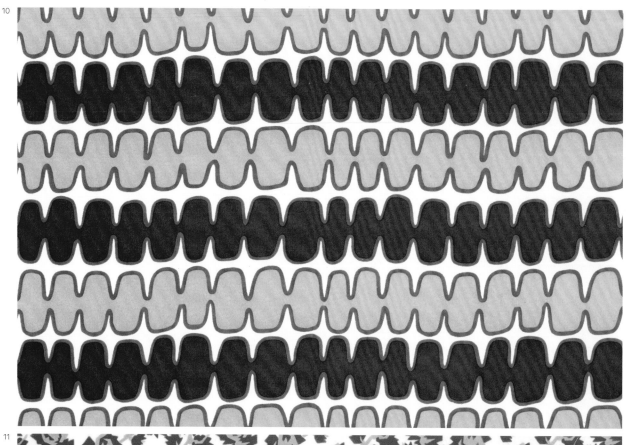

11

10. *'Fishbone' (S/S 2009).*
11. *'Mini Mean Roses' (S/S 2012).*
12. *'Bunny Dance' (A/W 2008).*
13. *'Marbles' (A/W 2002).*
14. *'Eye Eye Ivy' (S/S 2012).*
15. *'Magic Flowers' (S/S 2004).*

FORSTER ROHNER

A family-run business based in St Gallen, Switzerland, embroidery manufacturers Forster Rohner was founded in 1904 by Conrad Forster-Willi as Forster Willi & Co. Since the 1940s the company has collaborated with leading couturiers, such as Christian Dior and Cristóbal Balenciaga, resulting in a major pattern and photographic archive containing more than 400,000 embroidery designs from the label's one hundred-year history. Using advanced technologically refined solutions, the company continues to supply embroideries for contemporary designers of lingerie, prêt-a-porter and haute couture, including Prada, Valentino, Louis Vuitton, Calvin Klein, Chloé, Christopher Kane, Erdem and Thakoon. In addition, collections bearing the Forster Willi and Forster Rohner labels are presented biannually in Milan, Paris, London and Barcelona. Today the business is run by Emanuel and Caroline Forster, great-grandchildren of the company founder.

SCHIFFLI EMBROIDERY

Also known as Swiss embroidery, schiffli embroidery utilizes the combination of a continuously threaded needle and a shuttle containing a bobbin of thread. There are various processes producing a variety of effects, resulting in enormous flexibility with which to follow fashion trends.

01. *Satin stitch in guipure.*
02. *Schiffli-embroidered tulle with shaped edges.*
03. *Schiffli-embroidered tulle with shaped edges.*

following pages
04. *Guipure embroidery.*

pages 140-1
05. *Embroidered all-over frill.*
06. *Chenille guipure embroidery.*
07. *Schiffli-embroidered tulle with shaped edges.*
08. *Cellophane yarn fringes on tulle.*

01

04↓

FREYELLI

For inspiration, Ellie Hipkin focuses on the wild flora and fauna of the coastal strand, from the beaches to the South Down hinterland of the southern coast of England, where her textile design studio is based. Hipkin launched the Freyelli label after twelve years as a practitioner in the fashion industry, employed as a print designer in the mass production supply chain, where she worked with

leading high street manufacturers. In contrast, she now produces artisan pieces as uniquely crafted items or as part of a limited collection. Encompassing low- and high-tech approaches, Hipkin both hand-paints directly onto silk and also develops her designs to be printed digitally by the metre. Freyelli textiles are used for niche collections of tops, dresses and accessories.

DIGITAL PRINTING

Although digitally printed, the floral motifs appear as if they are constrained by a technique used for painting on silk, when gutta (a latex resist) is used to draw the outline of the picture to control the spread of dyes.

01. *Flower and feather digitally printed on silk (2012).*
02. *Blue flower print digitally printed on cotton (2012).*
03. *Placement print of blue flower digitally printed on silk (2012).*

01

02

PAINTING ONTO SILK
Painting freely by hand directly onto the silk enables the designer to create the qualities inherent in watercolour painting: a translucent wash of colour that bleeds into the surrounding area.

04. *'Waterfall Daisy' hand-painted on silk (2013).*
05. *'The Freya Flower' hand-painted on silk (2013).*
06. *'The Love Peacock' hand-painted on silk (2013).*
07. *'Watercolour Flowers' hand-painted on silk (2013).*
08. *'The Freya Flower' hand-painted on silk (2013).*

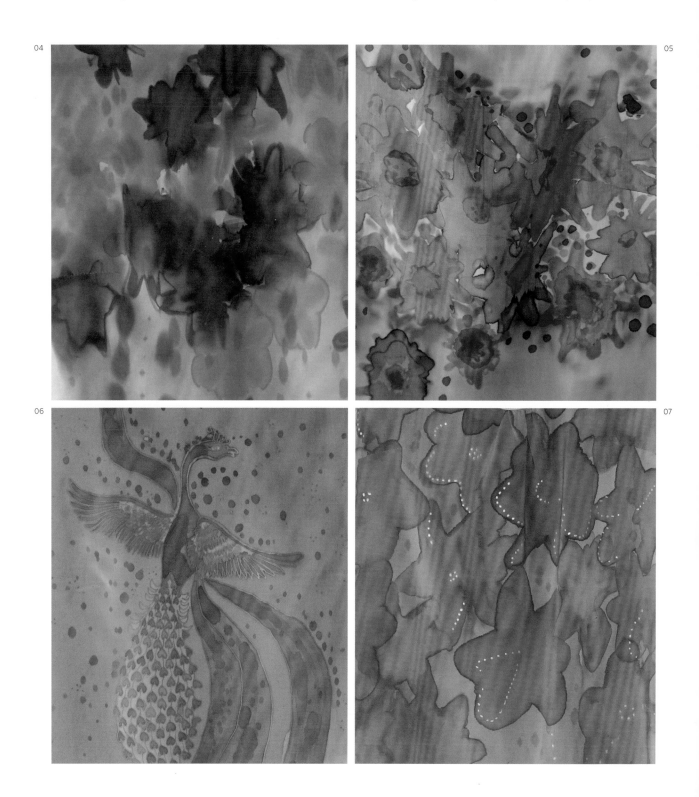

FURPHY SIMPSON*

Val Furphy and Ian Simpson met while studying at the Royal College of Art in London and set up Furphy Simpson after graduating in 1976. Initially designing and printing exclusive lengths of fabric for London-based fashion designers, the design duo then started to sell their designs internationally to all levels of the market, including couture. Exhibiting regularly at trade fairs in Paris, Frankfurt and Como, the company is mentioned frequently in many

DISCHARGE PRINTING

Furphy Simpson has been a leading exponent of the handcrafted discharge-printing process since the early 1990s. Usually using dark coloured dischargeable grounds, which are a feature of the Furphy Simpson aesthetic, they have used brighter coloured grounds (seen in swatches **02** and **04**) for spring/summer scarves.

01. *Discharge-printed patchwork crêpe de Chine squares sewn together for own label scarf design.*
02. *Discharge-printed patchwork crêpe de Chine squares sewn together for own label scarf design.*

publications and trade journals. Furphy Simpson has remained exclusive and the two founders carry out all the design work themselves. In 2012 they ceased producing print designs to concentrate on a unique luxury scarf collection. Many of the scarves are limited-edition 'works of art' and the fabrics are created using the discharge technique because the designers prefer this traditional skill and the enhanced quality that can be achieved with this process.

03. *A mix of photographic imagery taken from antique documents mixed with drawing for own label scarf design on silk twill.*
04. *'Hands-on' techniques such as cut-paper stencils, a waxy drawn line and hand-painting for own label scarf printed on silk twill.*
05. *A mix of photographic imagery taken from antique documents mixed with drawing for own label scarf design on silk twill.*

01

02

03

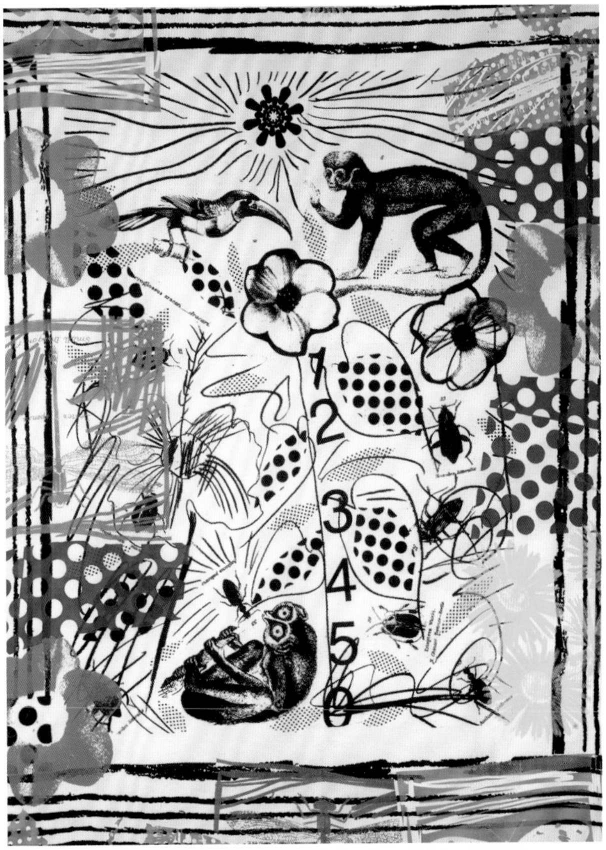

04

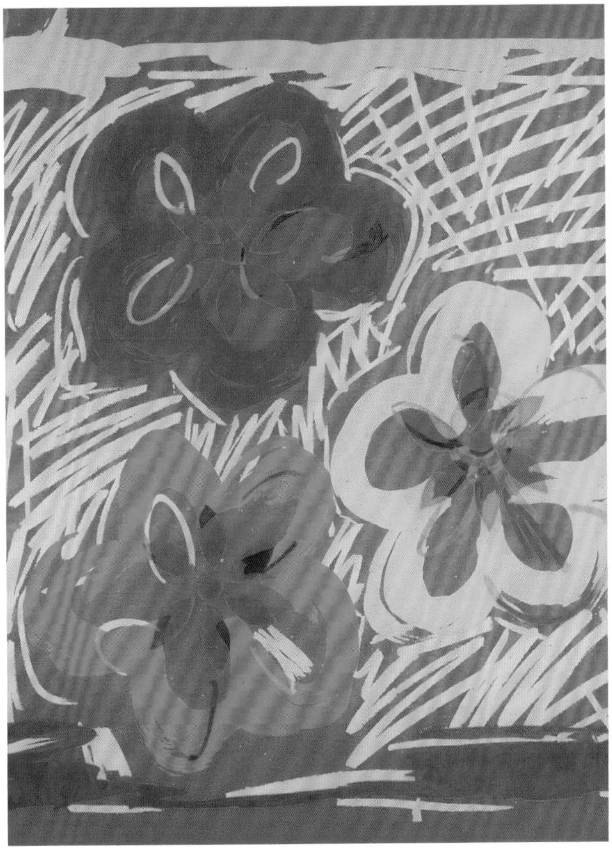

05

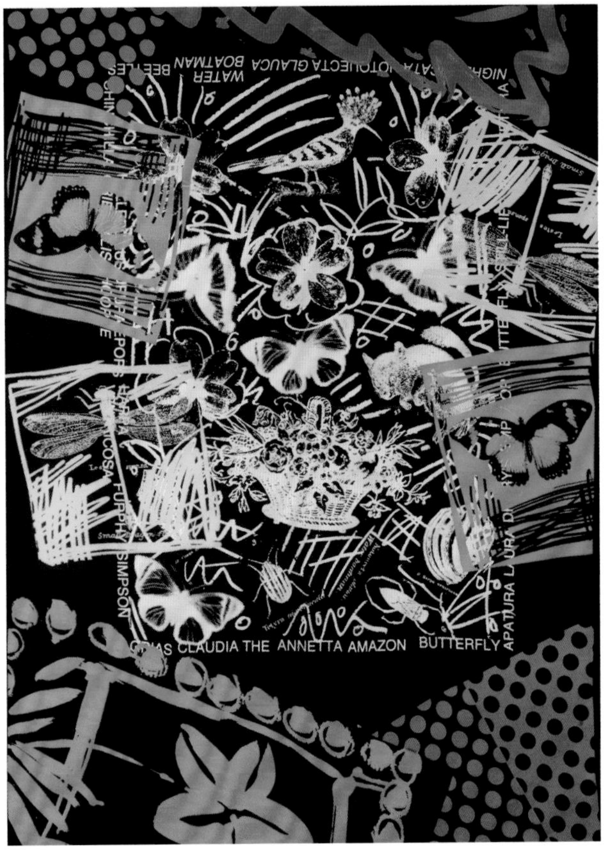

06

07

FURPHY SIMPSON FOR BURMA BIBAS

06. *An old Indian woodblock was used for the 'white' discharge with colours painted on later. Print on sandwashed silk for men's shirting (mid-1990s).*

07. *Design created using a potato cut, a cut-paper stencil and a tjanting tool for a print on sandwashed silk for men's shirting (mid-1990s).*

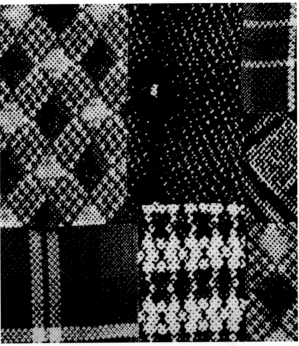

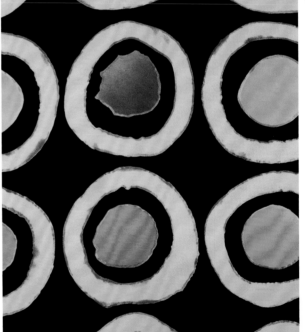

FURPHY SIMPSON FOR EQUIPMENT

08. *Pure colour discharge and hand-painted design out of a dark ground on silk for men and women's shirting (mid-1990s).*

09. *Patchwork tweed discharge print on silk for men and women's shirting (mid-1990s).*

10. *Patched together squares and rectangles of printed crêpe de Chine. The pale mint green is a result of the discharge paste being overlapped by an acid dye. Printed on silk for men and women's shirting (mid-1990s).*

11. *The halo around the colour is indicative of a discharge print and a result of the print recipe and the time the fabric would have been steamed. Printed on silk for men and women's shirting (mid-1990s).*

FURPHY SIMPSON FOR BYBLOS

12. *Blocks of dischargeable colour are laid down with 'white'*
florals and leaves on top discharged out. Printed on viscose
for men's shirting (S/S 1991).

12

13

FURPHY SIMPSON FOR CERRUTI 1881

13. *Scarf design inspired by an ancient map of the world and*
drawn with pen and ink, printed on silk georgette (1990s).

FURPHY SIMPSON FOR FENN, WRIGHT AND MANSON

14. *Monotone design on silk created using a paper
cut-out stencil placed on the screen and discharged
out (mid-1990s).*

FURPHY SIMPSON FOR MATSUDA

15. *Patchwork print on heavy rayon, steamed with a hot iron,
creating the ochre colour (mid-1990s).*

FURPHY SIMPSON FOR NICOLE FARHI

16. *Imagery taken from wrought iron for a mustard silk shirt (early 1990s).*

17. *Inspired by an image of the statues around the Paris Opera, manipulated using the Rauschenberg technique (early 1990s).*

18. *Painted on paper and then bleached out with large household paintbrushes (early 1990s).*

19. *Worked on handmade Japanese paper with dischargeable dyes using household bleach to discharge out the potato-cut motif (early 1990s).*

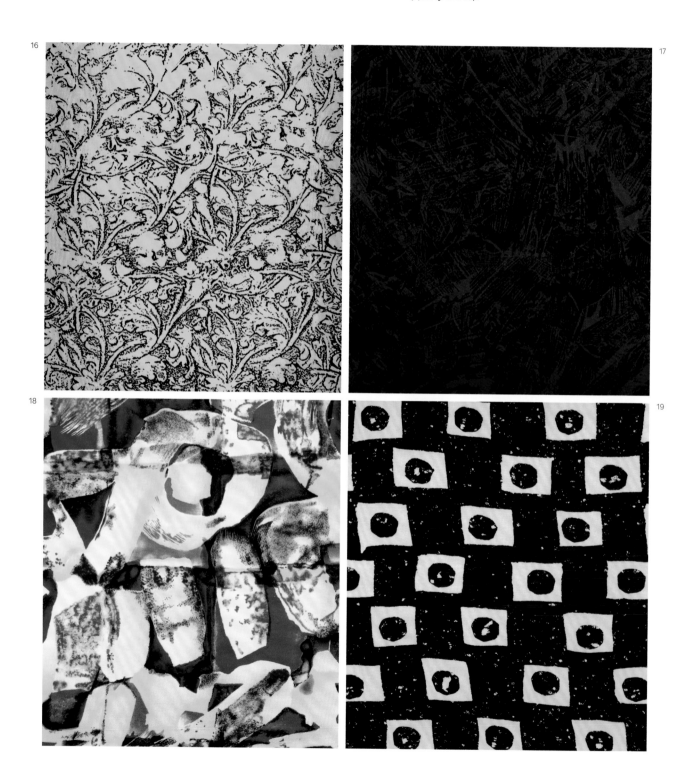

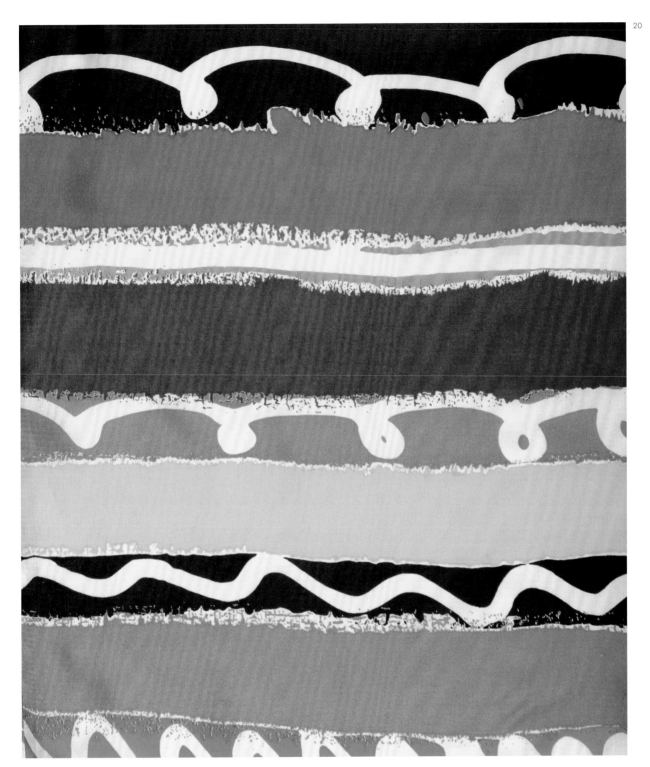

FURPHY SIMPSON FOR PLANET

20. *Colour discharge dyes painted in irregular stripes followed by white discharge applied over the top with a tjanting tool on sandwashed silk (S/S 1995).*

21

22

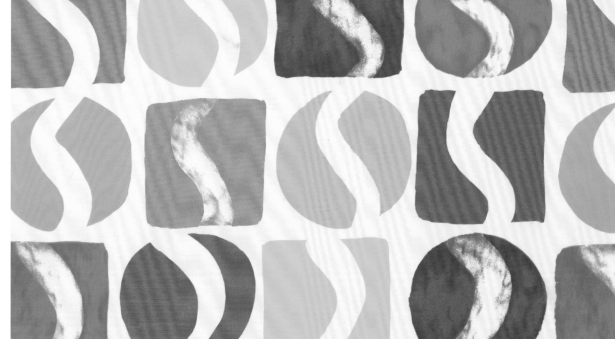

FURPHY SIMPSON FOR SPORTMAX

21. *Design created on paper with dyes and bleach printed on linen and viscose (S/S 1992).*

22. *Design created on paper with dyes and bleach printed on lightweight crêpe de Chine (S/S 1992).*

FURPHY SIMPSON FOR JAMS WORLD

23. *Ian Simpson placed his hands into discharge paste and laid them directly onto the fabric. Hawaiian shirt design on crinkled rayon.*

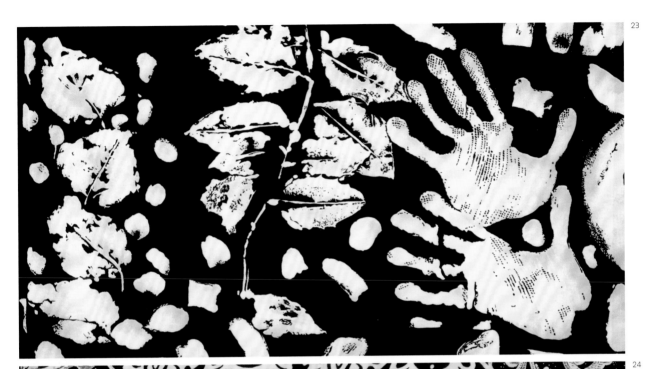

23

24

FURPHY SIMPSON FOR WINDSMOOR

24. *A multimedia print created using Indian woodblocks, photographic screens and drawing (late 1990s).*

GILES

Since launching his own label in 2003, British-born designer Giles Deacon has brought an irreverent and playful approach to his designs, most notably through his original prints and illustrations. Influenced by nature and the animal kingdom, as well as mythology and traditional craft, he has become widely admired for his beautiful and enigmatic jacquards. As a student at London's Central Saint Martins College of Arts and Design, he forged a close relationship with renowned British stylist Katie Grand. In 1998, they launched Giles's first collection for Milanese luxury brand Bottega Veneta. The designer also worked with Gucci and Jean-Charles de Castelbajac, before returning to London to focus on his own label. He was awarded British Fashion Designer of the Year in 2006, and in 2009 won the prestigious French ANDAM award.

TECHNIQUE

Before and since the Industrial Revolution, advances in textile technology have been spurred by a desire to produce opulent fabrics with rich patterning. In weaving, this prompted tapestry and handmade brocades; later the draw loom and jacquard system evolved.

01. *Banded sateen colour jacquard for an agitated bias stripe (A/W 2004).*
02. *Brocade of wheat ears, mice, crickets and toadstools (A/W 2004) .*
03. *Graphic bee and honeycomb colour jacquard (S/S 2005).*
04. *Weft-faced satin brocade with spiny graphic lattice (A/W 2007).*

01
→02

03

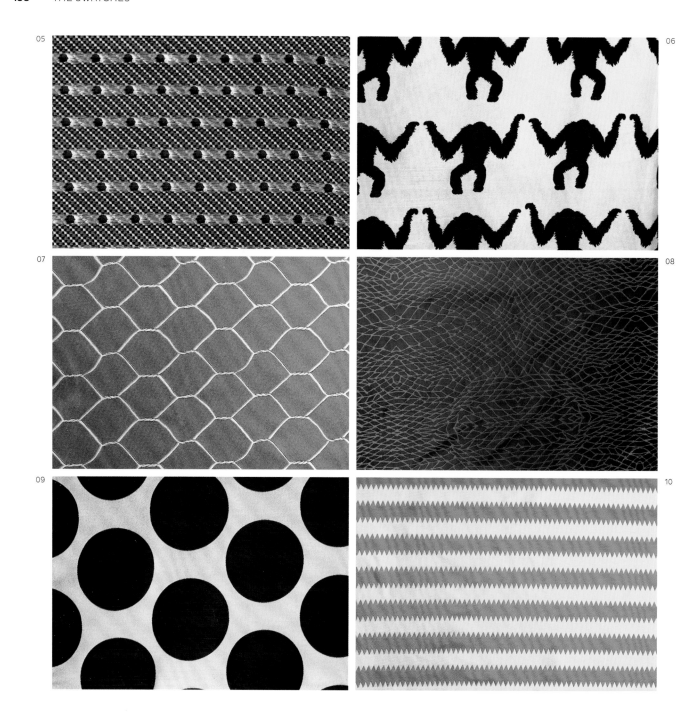

05. *Reverse of colour-dot and twill cloth used as obverse face (S/S 2006).*

06. *Chimpanzee chains in satin and jute (S/S 2005).*

07. *Satin jacquard chicken-wire mesh on tabby-weave ground (S/S 2006).*

08. *Spidery reversible sateen jacquard web on a tabby weave (A/W 2005).*

09. *Bold polka-dot sateen jacquard (A/W 2006).*

10. *Serrated jacquard sateen stripe (S/S 2005).*

11. *Psychedelic snails and roses on a tonally banded jacquard (A/W 2004).*

12. *Jacquard brocade lattice of cartoon gems and pearls (S/S 2005).*

following pages

13. *Colour jacquard rendition of butterfly scales and markings (A/W 2009).*

11

12

HAND & LOCK*

The elite embroidery house Hand & Lock was created in 2001. This was the result of a merger between the long-established M. Hand & Co., which was founded in 1767 and specialized in intricate goldwork for the military and royalty, and London-based company S. Lock Ltd., which was set up by Stanley Lock in 1956 when he took over the embroidery business of C. E. Phipps and Co., founded in 1898. S. Lock achieved international recognition for almost half a century working with well-known couturiers such as Christian Dior, Norman Hartnell and Hardy Amies. Royal commissions included gowns for Queen Elizabeth II, the late Queen Mother and Princess Diana. Hand & Lock continues to provide hand embroidery for niche markets, from civilian and military regalia through to ecclesiastical garments and couture, including collaborations with Chanel, Burberry, Louis Vuitton, Stella McCartney and Alexander McQueen.

GOLDWORK

Hand & Lock is renowned for its goldwork: a form of embroidery using metal threads. In this genre, the company exploits a wide variety of materials and techniques, but there are two important types of thread that are used in specific ways. 'Passing' is made of thin strips of metal wound around a core of cotton or silk attached by couching. 'Bullion' or 'Purl' thread comprises coils of metal, stretched slightly apart and couched through the gaps or cut up and applied like beads.

01. *Pomegranate detail in couched cordonnet gimp, beads and satin stitch, commissioned by Louis Vuitton (A/W 2013).*

02. *Tambour work of flowing couched cords, swathes of paillettes, French knots and chain stitch (February 2012).*

03. *Tambour work of ranked ruby beads, knotting and loose masses of metal paillettes (February 2011).*

04. *Sea urchin cluster rendered in white bugle beads, tipped with black beads (October 2012).*

following pages

05. *Sumptuous beaded surface from plaited threaded strands for Gavin Douglas (March 2009).*

06. *Interwoven eruptive surface of mossy chain stitch and gunmetal bugle beads and plates (April 2010).*

07. *Tonal needle-painting – or silk shading stitch – for the Khalid Al Qasimi collection (July 2008).*

pages 166–7

08. *Prince of Wales feathers in heraldic goldwork of silver and gold bullion thread on damask ground (January 2006).*

09. *Armorial bearing in high-relief ceremonial goldwork with raised bullion thread and paillettes (November 2012).*

10. *Christian Dior garlanded and crowned monogram badge in raised work of silk cordonnet gimp (S/S 2013).*

11. *Elaborate Burberry goldwork crest in raised silver, copper and gold bullion threads (A/W 2007).*

01
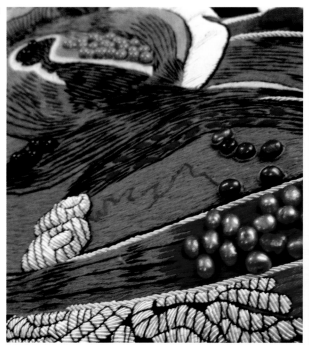

02

05

06

08

09

10

11

HELEN TURNER

A promulgator of knitwear with a contemporary edge, London-based designer Helen Turner began her exploration of knitted textiles at London's Chelsea College of Art and Design before studying fashion at the Royal College of Art while also working as an intern at Burberry and Céline. After graduating in 2011, Turner showed with Vauxhall Fashion Scout, an international showcase for fashion innovation and emerging design talent, and her work has featured in various publications. In 2011 she joined the design team at British heritage label Burberry. With an innovative approach to materials and structure that involves working with unusual yarns to build up complex textures, the designer is inspired by natural contours such as plaiting, weaving and knotting techniques.

MANIPULATING FIBRES

The yarns are integral to each design: threading, knotting and twisting to embellish and form the fabric. Hand-dyeing the yarns and then manipulating them while knitting enables the designer to create levels of rich fur-like textures.

01. *Coated cotton crochet (A/W 2012).*
02. *Nude silk knit with tassels (A/W 2012).*
03. *Symmetrical fur knit (A/W 2012).*

following pages
04. *Black cable knit with Swarovski crystal detail (A/W 2012).*

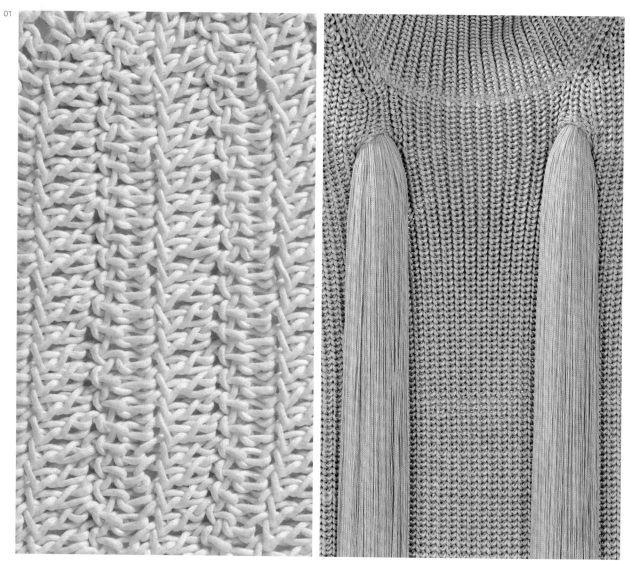

01

02

05

06

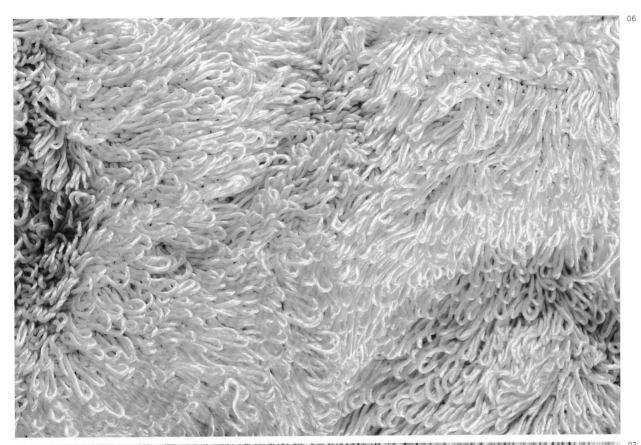

07

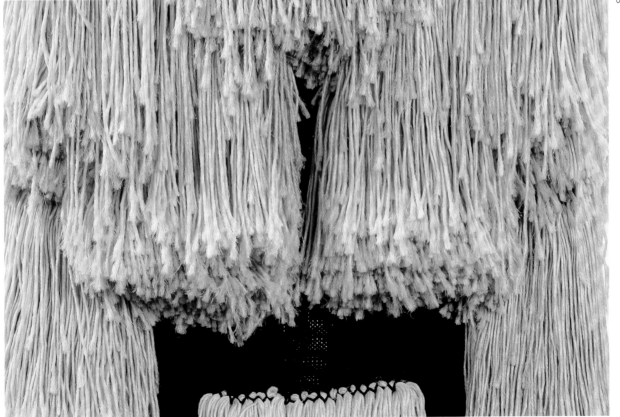

previous pages
05. *Nude silk knit with tassels and Swarovski detailing*
    (A/W 2012).
06. *Looped silk knit (A/W 2012).*
07. *Symmetrical hand-fringed skirt (A/W 2012).*

this page
08. *Chunky hand-knitted cable with fringing (A/W 2012).*
09. *Hand-knitted cables with fringing detail (A/W 2012).*
10. *Plaited yarn (A/W 2012).*

HOLLY FULTON

Scottish-born designer Holly Fulton combines strong graphic imagery and a use of bold colour with an obsessive preoccupation with surface detail, evidence of her previous experience in jewelry and accessory design. After completing a master's degree at London's Royal College of Art, Fulton worked as a womenswear and accessories designer at Parisian couture house Lanvin under the creative director Alber Elbaz. Two seasons showing her own collections at Fashion East, in 2009 and 2010, resulted in the designer winning the Swarovski Emerging Talent Award for accessories at the British Fashion Awards. Inspired by popular culture, Art Deco and Cubism, Fulton emphasizes texture and sculptural qualities, which often leads to three-dimensional elements being integrated into the fabric. The embellished prints are then configured into modern silhouettes with minimal construction detail.

REFLECTIVE PLASTIC LAMINATES
AND CRYSTAL CABOCHONS

Fulton incorporates crystal cabochons and nacreous shell laminates to provide intense surface decoration, enhancing the Art Deco sensibility and Cubist-inspired patterns of her textile designs.

01. *A mosaic of shell laminates (S/S 2012).*
02. *A graphic chequerboard marked with natural mother-of-pearl squares (S/S 2012).*
03. *Abstract zebra knit (S/S 2012).*
04. *Engineered digital print (S/S 2012).*
05. *Art Deco-inspired beaded and embellished print (S/S 2012).*

following pages
06. *Art Deco-inspired print enhanced with metal stud-work and hair on hide appliqué (S/S 2012).*

01
→02

03

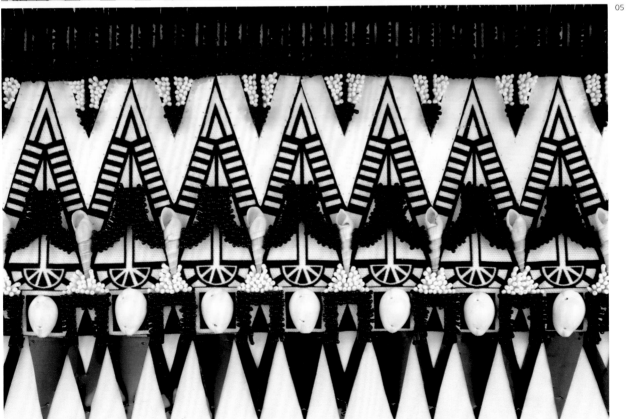

ENGINEERED DIGITALLY PRINTED TEXTILES

Featuring frequently in Holly Fulton's collections are engineered prints that are designed to fit the pattern piece. Further embellishment provides an emphasis on three-dimensional texture.

07. *All-over digital print on silk (S/S 2012).*
08. *Art Deco-inspired placement print (S/S 2011).*
09. *Engineered digital print (S/S 2012).*
10. *Engineered digital print (S/S 2011).*

11. *Graphic three-colour placement print (A/W 2010).*
12. *Engineered digital print (A/W 2011).*
13. *Monochrome all-over design digital print (A/W 2010).*
14. *Engineered digital print (S/S 2012).*
15. *Engineered digital print (S/S 2011).*
16. *All-over design digital print (A/W 2011).*
17. *Placement print with abstract zebra design with borders (S/S 2012).*
18. *All-over design digital print (S/S 2012).*
19. *Mirrored lips in an engineered digital print (A/W 2011).*

HOUSE OF HOLLAND

Suffused with tongue-in-cheek irony and an exuberant use of colour and pattern, House of Holland was launched by British designer Henry Holland in 2006 with the introduction of his rhyming slogan T-shirts, typically emblazoned with irreverent text such as 'I'll Tell You Who's Boss Kate Moss' and 'Get Yer Freak On Giles Deacon'. Holland studied journalism at the London College of Printing before embarking on a role as a stylist. With an astute instinct for publicity, the designer also forayed into marketing. In 2013 he appropriated an ice cream van – named 'Mr Quiffy' in reference to his trademark vertical quiff – as a travelling pop-up shop selling a House of Holland limited-edition collection to mark the relaunch of the label's e-commerce site. Holland's uniquely playful aesthetic is also evident in a range of eyewear and various collaborative projects, including H! by Henry Holland (a successful capsule collection for British high street store Debenhams, launched in 2010), Pretty Polly hosiery, and Superga.

TECHNIQUE

Holland transposes similar patterning across a range of fabrics, techniques and scales: the houndstooth check (**03**) appears digitally printed on silk, as a weave, embroidered and beaded, and as an intarsia knit.

01. *Vintage-inspired budgerigar and blossom print (A/W 2011).*
02. *Bingo counter spot repeat print (A/W 2011).*
03. *Houndstooth check print with colour transition (A/W 2012).*
04. *Bones and flowers print (Resort 2012).*
05. *Intarsia-knitted logo (Resort 2013).*
06. *Guatemalan-inspired rainbow bright stripes (Resort 2012).*
07. *Placement print in zigzag pattern (A/W 2012).*
08. *Monochrome interlocking bones print (Resort 2012).*
09. *Striped jersey knit with appliqué (A/W 2012).*
10. *Punk-inspired pins print (S/S 2012).*
11. *Large-scale bias plaid, screen-printed in glossy single shade on ridged tussah silk (S/S 2013).*

01

02

03
→04

05

06
→07

08

09
→10

11

HUSSEIN CHALAYAN

In his aeronautically engineered garments and animatronic dresses, Turkish-Cypriot-born designer Hussein Chalayan reveals himself as a resolutely conceptual innovator, discarding the demarcations between art, culture, technology and fashion. Subsidizing his creativity by simultaneously undertaking commercially led design output from 1993, Chalayan fronted the New York knitwear company TSE between 1998 and 2001 and was appointed fashion director to jeweler Asprey of London in 2001, launching his first collection for the company in 2003. Chalayan became the creative director of Puma Sportswear in 2008. Twice named Designer of the Year at the British Fashion Awards, in 1999 and 2000, he was also appointed a Member of the Order of the British Empire in 2006. Over the course of his career, numerous international museums and galleries have curated exhibitions of his design work, including five solo exhibits in Europe and Asia. He received the Lucky Strike Designer Award for lifetime achievements in 2012.

EMBROIDERY
Hand-embroidered contour satin stitch dissolves into flame satin stitch, creating a motion-blur effect engineered to the panel designs with the addition of laser-cut acrylic motifs (**10**).

01. *Holographic foil applied with heat processes to a smooth woven base cloth (S/S 2012).*
02. *Holographic foil applied with heat processes to a smooth woven base cloth (S/S 2012).*
03. *Holographic foil applied with heat processes to a smooth woven base cloth (S/S 2012).*
04. *Moiré silk satin plissé (S/S 2010).*

following pages
05. *'Crushed Car' digital print on jersey (S/S 2010).*
06. *Overprinted* fil coupé *jacquard figured lamé, with plain banding (S/S 2009).*
07. *Digital print shadow check on chiffon (S/S 2009).*
08. *Digital print on chiffon (S/S 2009).*
09. Trompe l'œil *photographic digital print of bundled clothes (S/S 2013).*

pages 188–9
10. *Embroidered yoke with double-edged punched leather trim (S/S 2012).*

01
→02

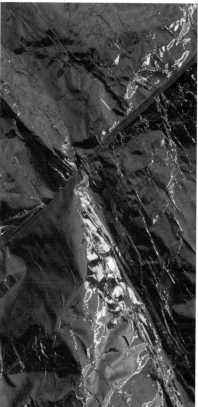

03

05

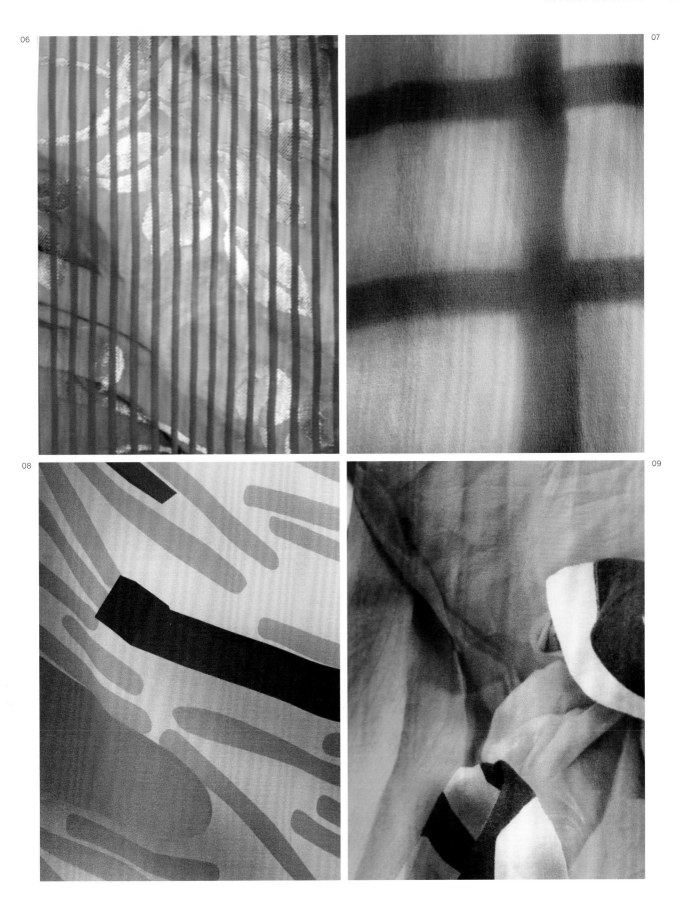

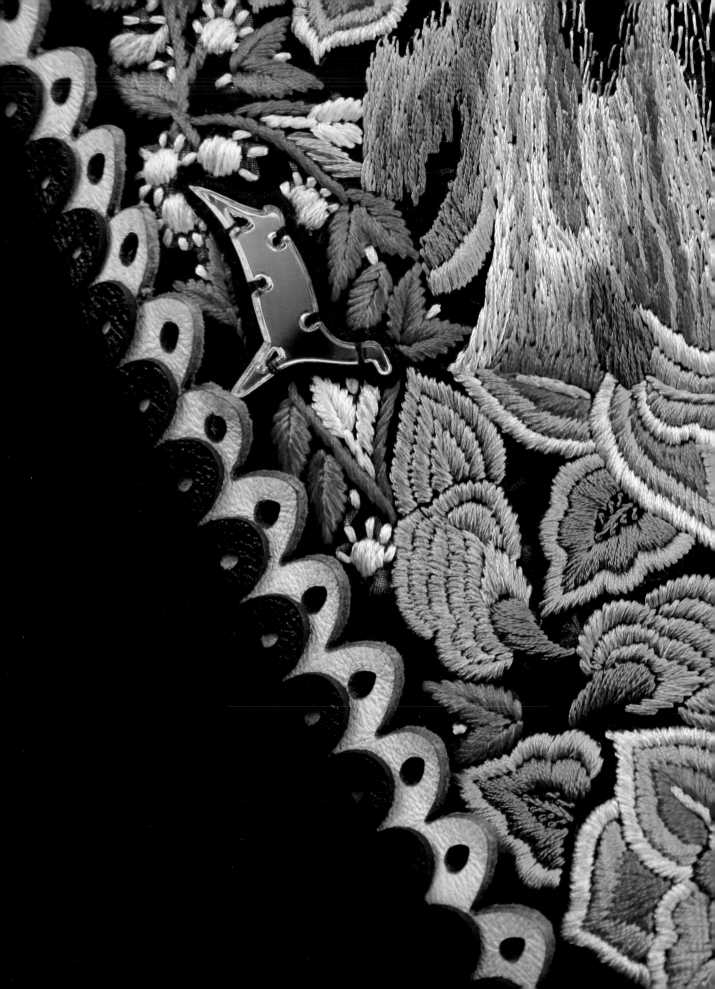

INSIDEOUT

Launched in 2004 by Denis James and Frances Yvette, Insideout is a label dedicated to digital-printing techniques that feature monochrome *trompe l'œil* motifs. The label was first showcased at an exhibition at Le Bon Marché in Paris and has subsequently won numerous awards, including the Premium Designer Award, Berlin, in 2011. The Victoria and Albert Museum in London commissioned the design duo to produce T-shirts for two exhibitions: 'Surreal Things' (2007) and 'Club to Catwalk' (2013). Since 2004, Insideout has printed super-real images on silk T-shirts, tops, dresses and shoes, creating pieces reminiscent of early London glam rock and punk as well as of Op art and 1950s dresses. Deconstructed shirts, 1970s denim, jewelled necklaces, distressed knitwear, laddered chiffon and sequin fabrics have all inspired the label and are digitally printed onto silk, denim and cotton jersey. Insideout is now retailed internationally including in Paris, London, New York, Moscow, Milan, Tokyo and Hong Kong.

PHOTO-REALIST DIGITAL PRINTING

The label utilizes digital printing to create *trompe l'œil* effects of various surfaces, particularly threadbare vintage items with all their imperfections and signs of wear. These are then surreally imposed onto the surface of a garment.

01. Trompe l'œil *crumpled chiffon, printed on silk (S/S 2009).*
02. Trompe l'œil *three-dimensional textured plastic, printed on silk (A/W 2009).*
03. Trompe l'œil *large spot folded fabric, printed on silk (S/S 2012).*
04. Trompe l'œil *laddered Fair Isle knitted fabric, printed on silk (A/W 2004).*
05. Trompe l'œil *side-lit quilted plastic, printed on silk (S/S 2011).*

01

02
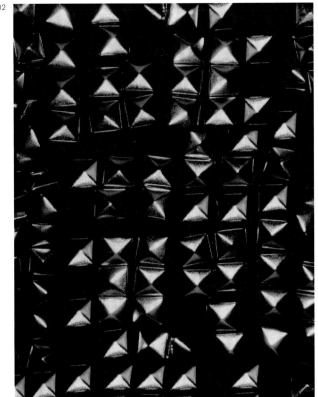

03

04

05
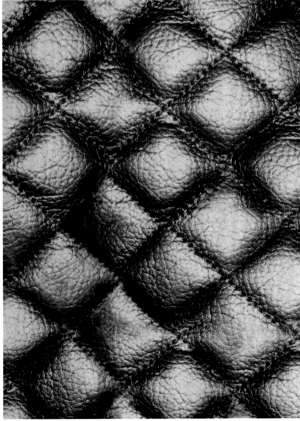

TROMPE L'OEIL

Trompe l'œil realism can be used to surreal effect when diaphanous materials are rendered on a substantial fabric.

06. Trompe l'œil *of creased tulle, printed on silk (S/S 2013).*
07. Trompe l'œil *rendering of three-dimensional zips in two dimensions, printed on silk (A/W 2009).*
08. Trompe l'oeil *pearl buttons forming the Union flag, printed on silk (A/W 2010).*

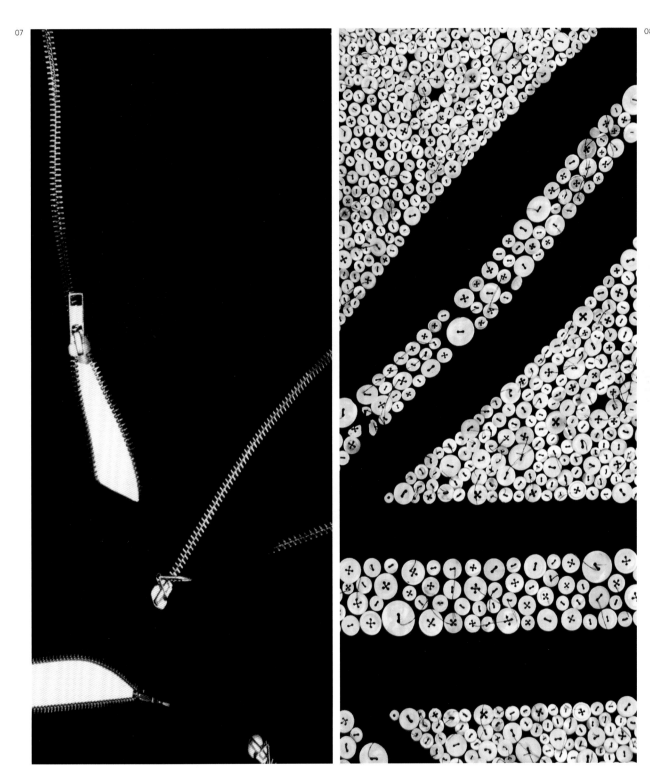

JAMES LONG

Initially established as a maker of menswear, British-born James Long added womenswear to his repertoire in a collection for Autumn/Winter 2011 presented by Fashion East, the nonprofit initiative established to nurture young designers. Long completed a master's degree in menswear and accessories at London's Royal College of Art in 2007, after which he worked for Virginia Bates before launching his own label in 2010. His collections are stocked in Harvey Nichols and in stores in New York, Paris, Los Angeles, Tokyo and Milan. Long's distinctive use of materials makes reference to sources that complement a controlled colour palette, including photography or the austere design ethos of the Bauhaus. This core aspect has extended to printing and finishing processes on other substrates, such as leather.

DISHEVELLED SURFACES
James Long produces collections that are characterized by the exploitation of the versatility of hand-knitting – and hand machine-knitting – to create rich, dishevelled surfaces.

01. *Scrollwork embroidery with chainette tape (S/S 2013).*
02. *Hand-machine-knitted stockinette with inlaid woven tapes (S/S 2013).*
03. *Warp-knitted spacer mesh, interlaced with bands of chainette and woven tape (S/S 2014).*

following pages
04. *Chunky hand-knit intarsia in plain and purl stitches (A/W 2013).*
05. *Digital print inspired by printing table backing cloths, replete with accidental stains (S/S 2011).*
06. *Graphic embroidery of beads, bugles and appliqué leather on reverse stockinette knit (A/W 2013).*

01

02

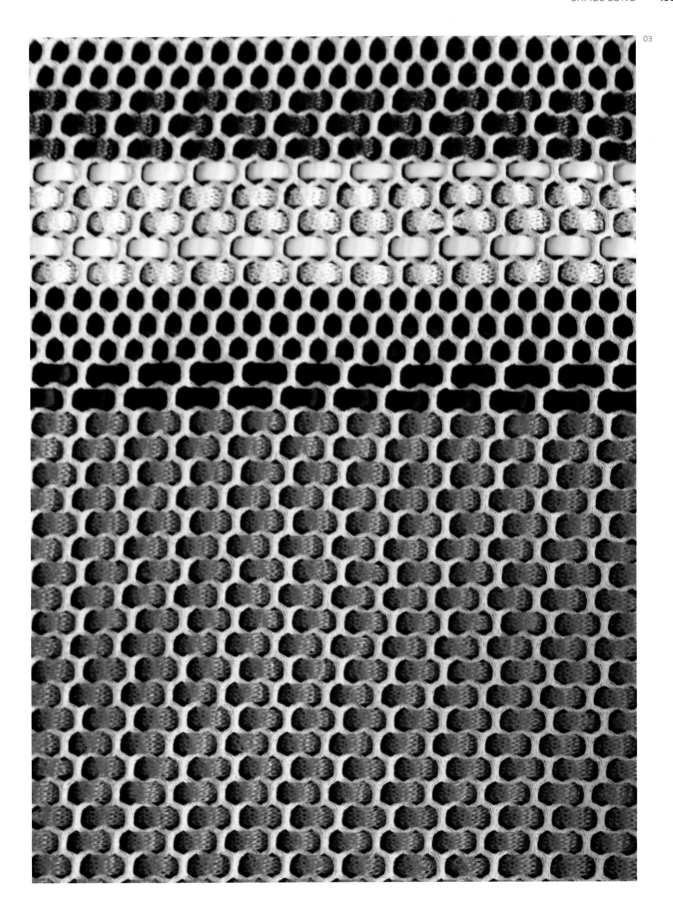

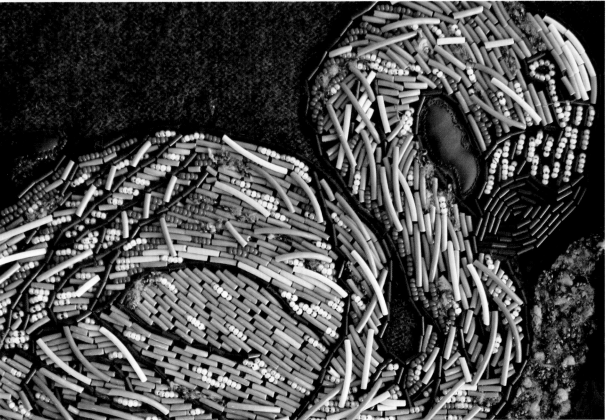

07

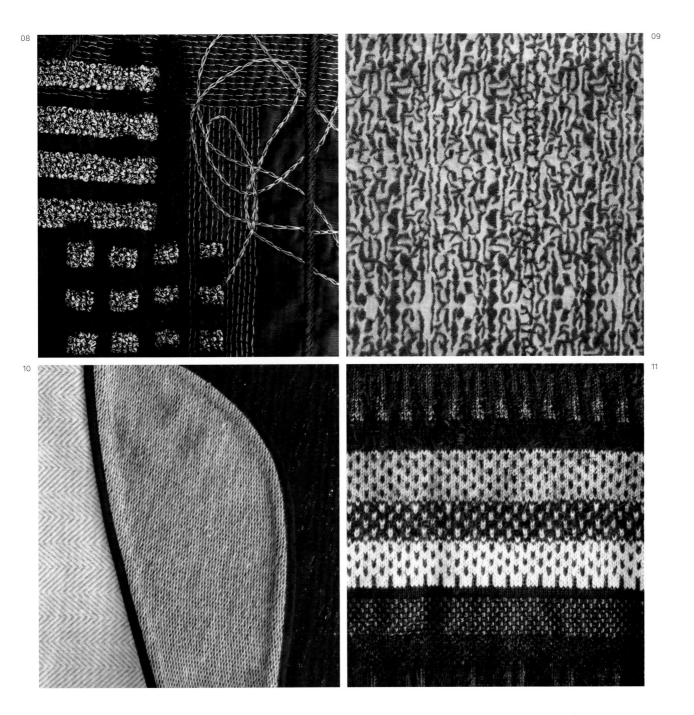

HAND TECHNIQUES

The use of tonal or monochrome combinations of print, yarn and fabric adds a graphic rigour to the fashion silhouette. Hand techniques are lavished on fabricating variegated surfaces from embroidery or by structuring knits.

07. *Linear overprint on suffused shirting check (Men S/S 2013).*

08. *Hand-embroidered montage on patterned, knitted base (Men S/S 2013).*

09. *All-over texture in machine-embroidered satin stitch on denim (Women A/W 2013).*

10. *Piped panels of herringbone twill, tabby weave and subtle dark lamé (Men S/S 2014).*

11. *Banded patterned and textured knit in wool and mohair (Women A/W 2013).*

JOHN ANGUS

John Angus is a designer and respected academic, based in the UK, with a consultant practice in fashion and textile design. His work in knitwear design development has spanned the transition from traditional artisanal methods and mechanical automation to the advent and universal adoption of digital manufacturing systems, which have reasserted knitting as the earliest form of additive manufacturing. As well as directing renowned degree programmes in fashion and textile design at various universities and pioneering the direct employment of advanced CAD/CAM systems by designers, Angus has worked for a quarter of a century with Italian manufacturers and design labels through his long-standing collaboration with a specialist knitwear practice, Studio Sabbatini. With its extensive client base, this studio demands a constant refreshment of its structural repertoire to enable differentiation between brands at the level of innovation and seasonal styling. Clients include labels such as Spirito, Hemmond, John Ashpool, Dunhill, Basile and Gabriella Frattini.

STRUCTURAL INTERPLAY OF TECHNIQUES

Many complex effects of colour patterning and texture are attained by the structural interplay of just two alternating yarns. These are fed to individual machine needles sequentially, using permutations of the core vocabulary of knitting stitch types: knit, miss (slip), tuck and transfer.

01. *Coarse-gauge knit using plain and purl faces and dropped stitches (2004).*
02. *Interlaced rib cabling in two tones, creating a faux woven surface (2004).*
03. *Figured plain and purl stitches, using plating feeder to give colour effect (2007).*
04. *Mock twill weave, constructed in two colours of plain face, knitted floats (2010).*
05. *Reversible micro-cabled herringbone twill in two colours of lambswool rib (2010).*
06. *Suffused geometric purl-patterning laddered stitch in alpaca and wool (2004).*
07. *Large-scale broken check in laddered purl fabric (2004).*
08. *Ladder-back chevron jacquard in monofilament polyester and cotton (2007).*
09. *Coarse-gauge knit with reversible banded tuck jacquard in cashmere (2005).*

following pages
10. *Three colours in single-row stripes with large, shot effect, tuck pattern (2010).*
11. *Twisted intarsia netting, held in groups by floating stripe insertion (2005).*

01

FRAGMENTED COLOUR

Effects of scintillation of colour can be attained through combining a small pattern with solid banding, through the striping of rich texture and colour mixes, or by fragmenting colour with textured pattern.

12. *Intarsia stripes on a small-scale false plain ground, creating a check (2003).*

13. *Purl-faced stripe with controlled space-dyed and textured yarn mixes (1993).*

14. *Striated three-colour relief jacquard pattern in laddered plain and purl (2009).*

15. *Tubular two-colour jacquard with pattern defined by external floats (2003).*

16. *Bias rib stripes, controlling engineered space-dyed yarn by partial knitting (2003).*

17. *Corded two-colour, two-faced twill in Shetland wool with 1 x 1 rib trim (2010).*

TECHNIQUE

The engineered intersection of areas of disparate colour forms part of the common means of creating impact between the techniques of both knitting and weaving, offering rich possibilities for the transfer and intermingling of effects.

18. *Fine-gauge cotton jersey in two-colour, geometric vertical stripe (2003).*

19. *Lambswool three-colour laddered jacquard, forming large suffused plaid (2004).*

20. *Reciprocating short-row intarsia, creating controlled space-dyed effect (1994).*

21. *Garter-stitch laddered micro-jacquard in three colours of alpaca and wool (2004).*

22. *Stable, tweed-effect coarse knit in richly blended wool and mohair yarns (2007).*

23. *Two-colour tartan knit in plain and purl transfer jacquard (2009).*

24

TECHNIQUE

Complex structure at a detailed scale is exploited to attain both surface texture and colour patterning with larger impact when electronic selection mechanisms are available. This is the key premium of the advent of digital sampling systems.

24. *Fine-gauge electronic jersey with shot colour patterning and relief effects (2009).*

25. *Three-colour diamond check pattern in relief tuck jacquard (2010).*

26. *Tubular jacquard pattern, with opposed monofilament and plated yarns (2008).*

27. *Multicoloured plush jacquard fabric in rich wool and alpaca yarns (2007).*

28. *Broken houndstooth check in laddered 'stripy-backed' jacquard (2007).*

29. *Coarse-gauge intarsia inserted into three-colour tuck jacquard (2007).*

30. *Multi-colour plated intarsia geometric in wool on monofilament ground (2003).*

JOHN SMEDLEY*

John Smedley is globally recognized for its fully fashioned fine-gauge luxury knitwear. Family-owned for 225 years, the John Smedley label not only utilizes production methods and handcrafted finishing techniques that have been passed down through the generations but also exploits modern technology. The factory was founded in 1784 by John Smedley and Peter Nightingale near Matlock in Derbyshire. Initially specializing in the spinning of cotton, the company first produced designed knitwear in the 1920s. John Smedley's

INTARSIA KNITTING TECHNIQUE

Through the use of the intarsia knitting technique, John Smedley added to its repertoire of plaids and stripes during the 1950s with the diamond (argyle) check, which became a wardrobe staple of men's leisurewear. The design of elongated diamonds in two colours has appeared in many different configurations (**05**).

'Isis' shirt, with a unique patented collar, was developed in the 1930s and would later become known as the polo shirt. Only natural fibres are used, including merino lambswool and Sea Island cotton, and in 2008 the company introduced the latest Shima technology. A capsule collection was launched in 2011, challenging traditional design through the use of the John Smedley whole garment machines: each garment is sculpted to mould to the body, producing an uncompromising fit with seamless perfection.

01. *Intarsia plaid, striated with plain knit 'draws' (A/W 2008).*
02. *Geometric float jacquard in plain black ground (S/S 2008).*
03. *Tonal stripe laterally distorted by transfer lace repetitions (S/S 2002).*
04. *Chevron attained by striping in* fléchage *(A/W 2008).*
05. *Pure intarsia in stocking stitch (S/S 2008).*
06. *Banded candy stripe in stocking stitch (S/S 2002).*

01

02

07

08

FULLY FASHIONED KNITWEAR

Throughout the history of knitwear manufacturing there has been a consumer preference for garments that are fashioned to shape (or fully fashioned). Traditionally this method was reserved for luxury fibres.

this page
07. *Alternating two-colour stripe disrupted by held stitches (S/S 2008).*
08. *Multicoloured diamond check produced on fine-gauge 'V' bed machinery (S/S 2008).*

following pages
09–19. *Decades of production of John Smedley knitwear have been characterized by the creation of multicoloured stripes in fully fashioned garments.*

09

10

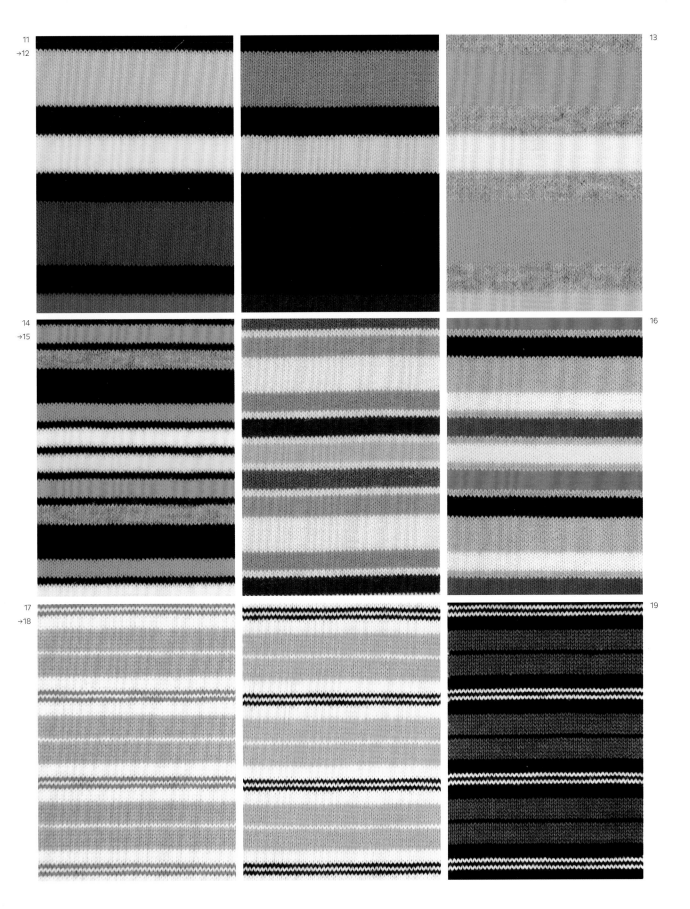

JOHNSTONS OF ELGIN

Globally recognized as the foremost purveyor of 'noble' yarns, vicuña and cashmere, Scottish heritage company Johnstons of Elgin was founded by Alexander Johnston in 1797. The factory was built on the banks of the River Lossie in north-east Scotland and was powered by the fast-running waters. In the early 1840s, the company created a range of Estate Tweeds, which were used to identify people who lived and worked in the same area. In the 1860s, Johnstons began exporting to Italy, France, Germany, Belgium, South America, Japan and later the USA, setting the precedent for 21st-century standards in manufacture. The company's long-standing record of export success was recognized in 2011 when it was awarded the prestigious UK Fashion and Textile Gold Award. In 2013 Johnstons was granted the Royal Warrant of Appointment. With clients including Savile Row tailors and contemporary designers, Johnstons also offers men's and women's ranges as well as textiles for interiors. Johnstons's knitwear is manufactured at its mill in the town of Hawick.

WOVEN TWEEDS

At the core of the richness of woven tweeds is the blending of colours of wool, prior to the spinning and weaving processes. Three or four separately dyed parcels of strong colour may be mixed and carded together in the woollen spinning system to create a subtle hue that reveals its depth at close examination. Similarly, the complex intertwining of warp and weft is used to create a rich visually textured ground against which stronger accent colours can play.

01. *100% pure new wool windowpane pin check in 4.5 x 4 cm repeat.*

02. *100% pure new wool windowpane pin check.*
03. *100% pure new wool windowpane pin check.*
04. *100% pure new wool Estate Tweed double overcheck.*
05. *100% pure new wool Estate Tweed overcheck in 7.5 x 6 cm repeat.*
06. *100% pure new wool Estate Tweed overcheck.*
07. *100% pure new wool Donegal fleck hopsack tweed.*
08. *100% pure new wool Donegal fleck hopsack tweed.*
09. *100% pure new wool herringbone tweed overcheck.*
10. *100% pure new wool Estate Tweed twin overcheck.*
11. *100% pure new wool hopsack overcheck.*
12. *100% pure new wool herringbone tweed overcheck.*

01
→02
03
04
→05
06

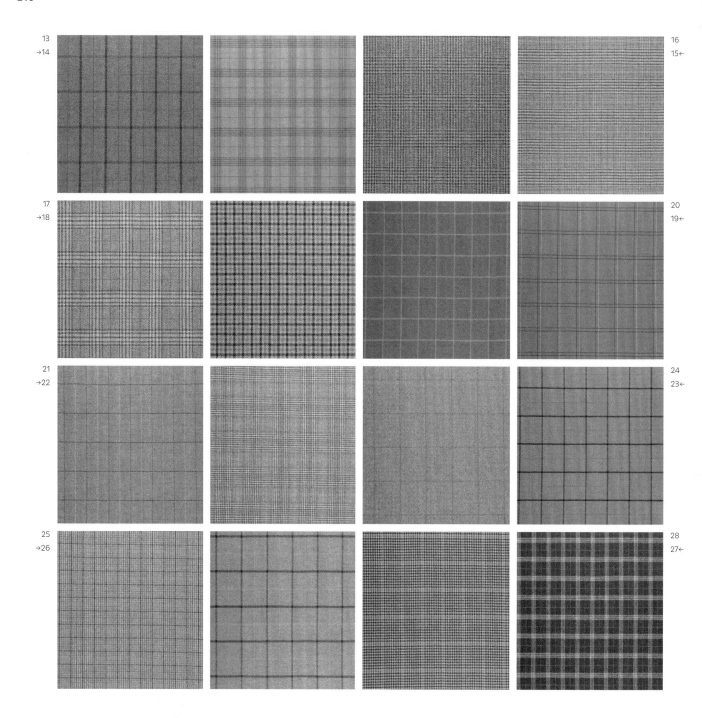

13. *100% pure new wool Estate Tweed double overcheck.*
14. *100% pure new wool Saxony overcheck.*
15. *100% pure new wool Prince of Wales check.*
16. *100% cashmere check.*
17. *100% pure new wool glen check.*
18. *100% pure new wool 6 x 6 cm check.*
19. *100% cashmere windowpane pin check.*
20. *100% pure new wool Saxony tramline overcheck.*
21. *100% pure new wool Saxony double overcheck*
in 7.5 x 6 cm repeat.

22. *100% pure new wool glen check.*
23. *100% pure new wool herringbone tweed with overcheck.*
24. *100% pure new wool Saxony double overcheck.*
25. *100% pure new wool fine houndstooth overcheck.*
26. *100% cashmere double overcheck.*
27. *100% cashmere houndstooth overcheck.*
28. *100% pure new wool Saxony box check.*
29. *100% cashmere houndstooth over check.*
30. *100% pure new wool box check in 4.5 x 4 cm repeat.*

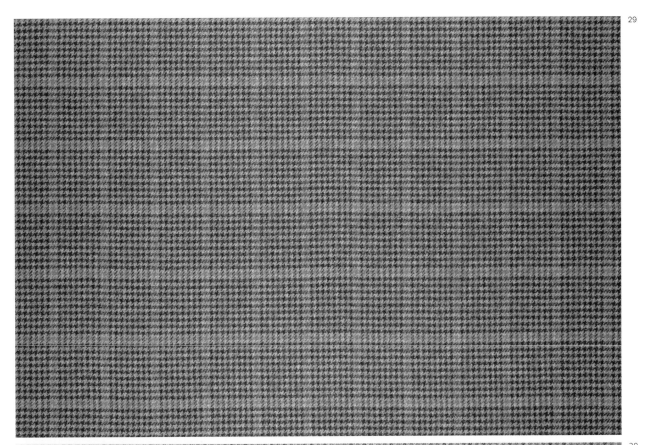

29

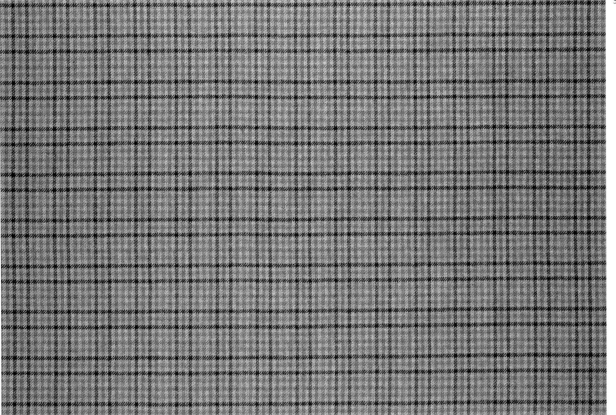

30

JONATHAN SAUNDERS

Scottish-born textile artist Jonathan Saunders was at the forefront of the 21st-century print revival when he debuted his finely judged yet kaleidoscopic prints in his graduate collection in 2002. The designer continued to show regularly at London Fashion Week until 2008, when he moved his collections to New York, returning to London in 2010. Saunders has designed successful capsule collections for British high street store Topshop, British department store Debenhams and US chain store Target/GO. In 2012 the designer expanded his label to include menswear, showing for the first time in Milan in 2012. More recently, Saunders has deployed his authoritative and nuanced use of colour away from print and into surface texture and structured garments.

ENGINEERED PRINT
Engineered to fill a dedicated space – the yoke of a dress, the hem of a skirt, across the shoulders – the hyper-coloured bird print (**03**) crosses the boundaries of the garment to garland the body with foliage.

01. *A graphic proposal for a three-colour basket-weave print inspired by the work of French architect and designer Charlotte Perriand (Pre-autumn 2012).*
02. *Digitally printed ombré on stretch georgette (A/W 2007).*
03. *Half-drop repeat of birds and foliage in teal (A/W 2011).*

following pages
04. *Panel with colour transition from black to green (A/W 2011).*
05. *A graphic proposal for garlanded blossoms in English blue (S/S 2011).*

pages 222–3
06. *Pugin-inspired wallpaper border print in fuchsia pink (Resort 2012).*

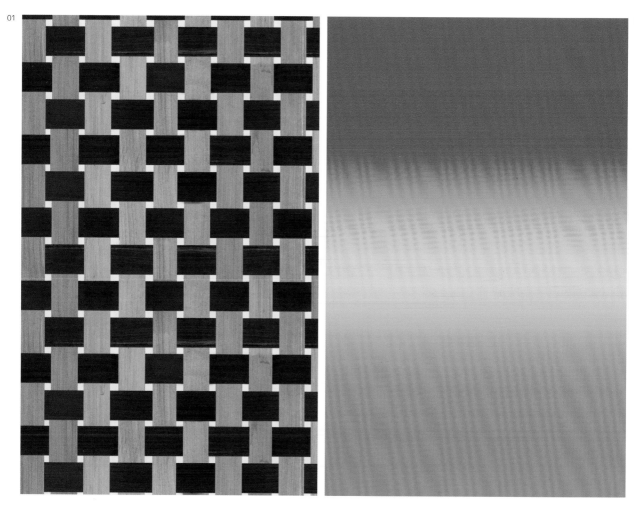

01

02

03

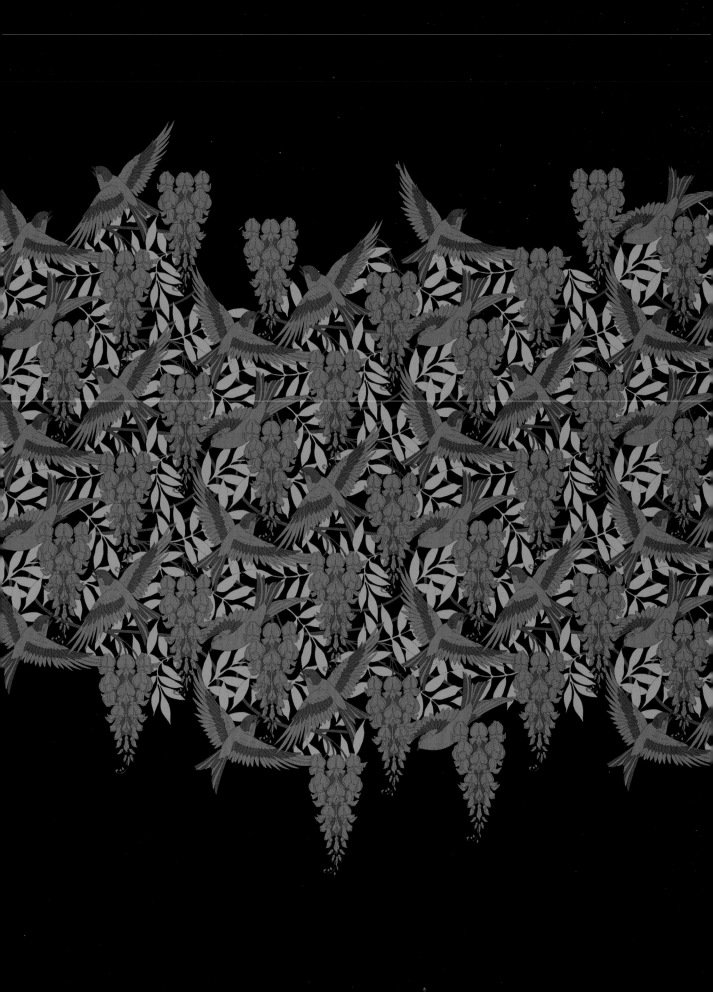

04

KAREN NICOL

Embroidery and mixed-media textile artist Karen Nicol brings unexpected materials and a new perspective to the traditional crafts of fabric embellishment. Her London-based design and production studio has been established for more than a quarter of a century and for many years she has designed for fashion as well as for interior products for global dignitaries such as the Emir of Qatar. Nicol specializes in Irish machine work, Cornelly work, beading and hand embroidery. Her wide range of clients has included many leading labels such as Marc Jacobs, Chloé, Vera Wang, John Rocha, Julien Macdonald, Betty Jackson, Matthew Williamson, Bruce Oldfield, Givenchy and Chanel. Nicol now creates 'couture creatures', shown at the Rebecca Hossack art galleries in London and New York.

MACHINE EMBROIDERY

The art of embellishing cloth by hand or machine can be achieved by many methods. All of the swatches have been produced on the Irish machine, a simple industrial embroidery machine with a swing needle and knee peddle.

01. *'George And The Dragon'. Silk organza with thick braids couched down with an Irish machine into frogging (A/W 2005).*
02. *Satin stitch flowers and photo-realist woollen embroidered inserts worked freehand on the Irish machine and then a lace cut by hand (A/W 2005).*
03. *Lace made with couched soutache braids and regimental ribbon (A/W 2005).*
04. *Lace created with a rolled raffia interspersed with embroidered raffia flowers (A/W 2005).*
05. *Lace made of couched vintage braid with three-dimensional flowers and birds (A/W 2005).*

01

02

03

04

05

LEWIS & LEWIS DESIGN

Jaqui Lewis established Lewis & Lewis Design in 1991 after many years working in partnership with other designers. This small London-based studio produces fashion print designs with a design ethos led by creativity, individuality and innovation combined with a strong awareness of international trends. The company exhibits biannually at Indigo, Paris, and designs sell globally from the USA to South Korea, Australia, Brazil and Turkey, as well as throughout Europe. The company's digital prints have been seen on the catwalks at Etro, Marni and Dries Van Noten. Each season Lewis & Lewis Design produces two collections, which are constantly updated according to global trends. The designers focus on attention to detail to create a range of unique textiles.

DIGITAL PRINTING
Over the past ten years, the studio has developed from a base of hand-painting all the designs directly on cloth to drawing, scanning and working on the computer to produce digital designs required by contemporary clients.

01. *Complex banded monochrome digital print by Vicky Emby (S/S 2011).*
02. *Geometric grid with humorous silhouettes by Vicky Emby (S/S 2009).*
03. *Photo-realist geometric print from running-stitch embroidery by Justine Stansall Seiler (S/S 2009).*

following pages
04. *All-over impressionistic floral print by Vicky Emby (S/S 2008).*
05. *Monochrome rose bouquet print by Jaqui Lewis (A/W 2011).*
06. *Tendrils of interlocking foliage in a monochrome print by Helen Race (S/S 2010).*

01

02
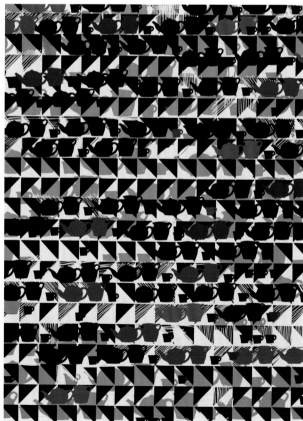

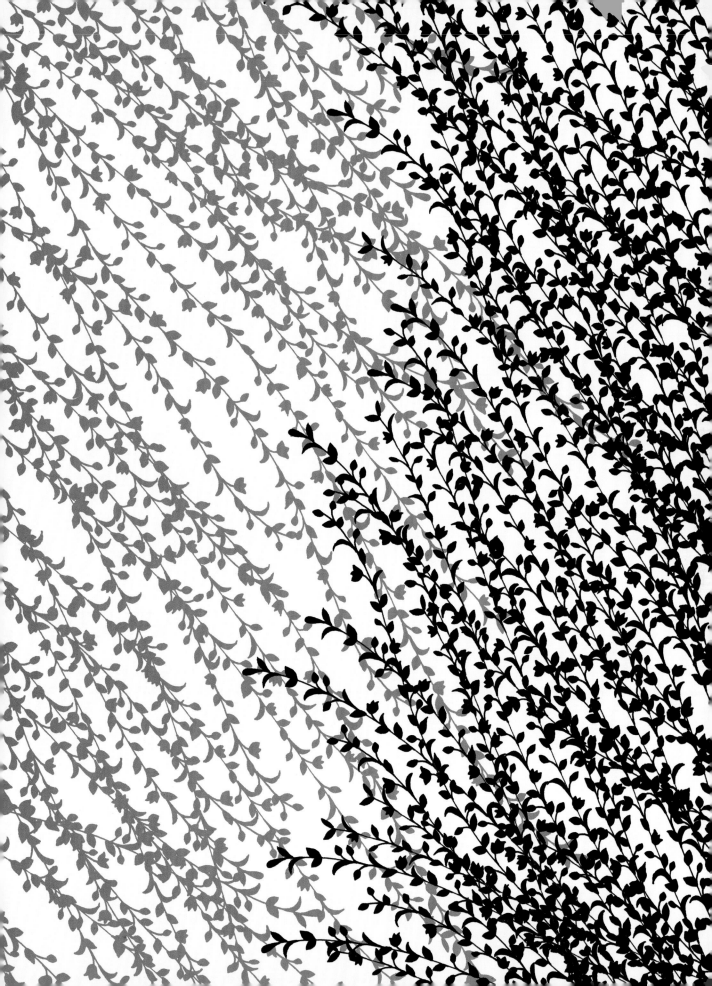

08

09

10

11

07. *Graphic florals in Fauvist colours by Danielle Saletes (A/W 2010).*

08. *Painterly flowers and foliage by Vicky Emby (S/S 2011).*

09. *Layers of block-coloured florals with border accents by Bryony Hart (A/W 2010).*

10. *Garlanded small-scale florals layered over loose brushstrokes by Bryony Hart (S/S 2011).*

11. *Delicately realistic floral border print by Danielle Saletes (S/S 2011).*

following pages

12. *Border print of cascading beads by Jaqui Lewis (A/W 2011).*

13. *All-over filigree of layered bead strands by Bryony Hart (S/S 2011).*

pages 234–5

14. *Blurred mosaic by Bryony Hart S/S 2010).*

15. *Diagonal digital scraffiti stripes by Jaqui Lewis (S/S 2012).*

16. *Digital scraffiti over layered spheres by Vicky Emby (S/S 2008).*

12

13

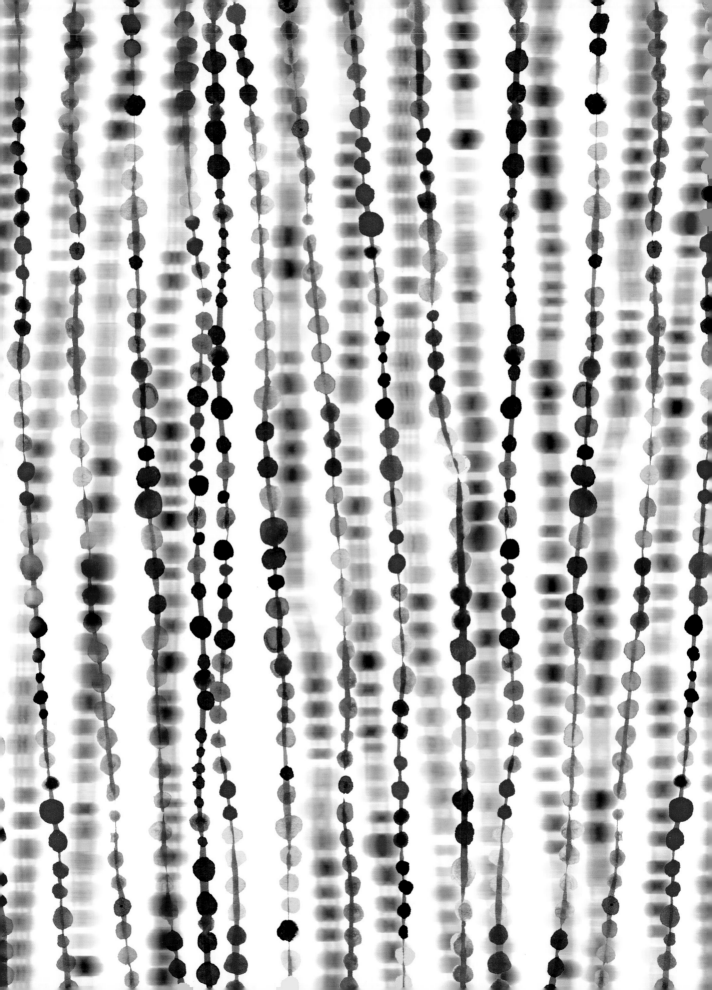

14

15

16

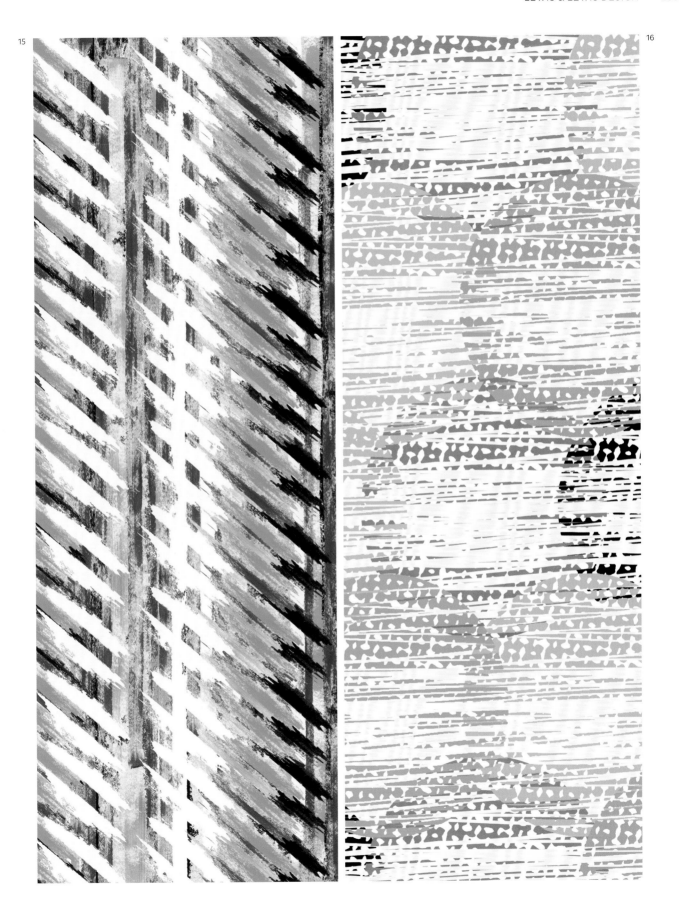

LIBERTY

Since it was founded by Arthur Lasenby Liberty in 1875, the London store Liberty has been a luxury emporium at the forefront of the decorative arts. By 1890, the company was known as Liberty & Co., purveyor of 'artistic' dress and interiors in the Art Nouveau style, one of the design aesthetics with which the company continues to be associated. During the 20th century, Liberty consolidated its role as the leading store for quality decorative textiles with collaborations with innovative print designers, including Lucienne Day, Bernard Nevill and Collier Campbell. More recently, Liberty has enjoyed associations with labels such as Marc Jacobs and Nike. No longer in family ownership, the company is majority-owned by BlueGem Gamma Limited. In 2005 a new brand was launched: 'Liberty of London'. The brand was renamed and relaunched in 2010 under 'Liberty London'.

TANA LAWN

One of the fabrics in the vast range offered by Liberty is Tana lawn, a fine lightweight cotton. The original Tana lawn fabric patterns were created in the early 1930s. William Haynes Dorell was a cotton buyer and created the name Tana lawn for an existing cotton lawn base. During this period the buyers commissioned the patterns, but the designs were by top design companies such as Silver Studio. Tana lawn fabrics were some of the key block-printed textiles produced in Liberty's Merton Abbey Mills print works, London.

01. *'Wiltshire'. The densely patterned leaf and berry design was designed for Liberty in 1933 and reintroduced in 1968.*
02. *'Wiltshire'. A classic Tana lawn in an alternative colourway.*
03. *'Poppyland'. Art Nouveau-inspired printed cotton (1904).*
04. *'Felicite'. Dispersed floral motifs in Tana lawn (1933).*
05. *'Cathryn's'. Overlapping stylized florals on a white ground.*
06. *'Felix Raison'. Originally based on a traditional paisley shawl from the 1850s, the design has been redrawn by the Liberty Art Fabrics design studio.*
07. *'Wild At Heart'. Designed by Amanda Harrison in Tana lawn (A/W 2013).*
08. *'Carline'. A 1950s-inspired graphically elegant print (1994).*
09. *'Sophie's Blossom'. Created by in-house studio from a drawing by Bridget Carey, aged nine.*
10. *'Langley'. Inspired by Odilon Redon's painting* Ophelia among the Flowers *(1905–8) (S/S 2012).*
11. *'Mitsi'. Recreated from a design in the archive by the Liberty Art Fabrics design studio, this print evokes Liberty's long association with Japanese style. The original was designed by a member of the studio in the 1950s (S/S 2013).*

01
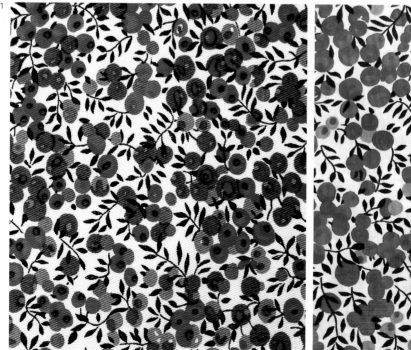

02

03
→04

05

06
→07

08

09
→10

11

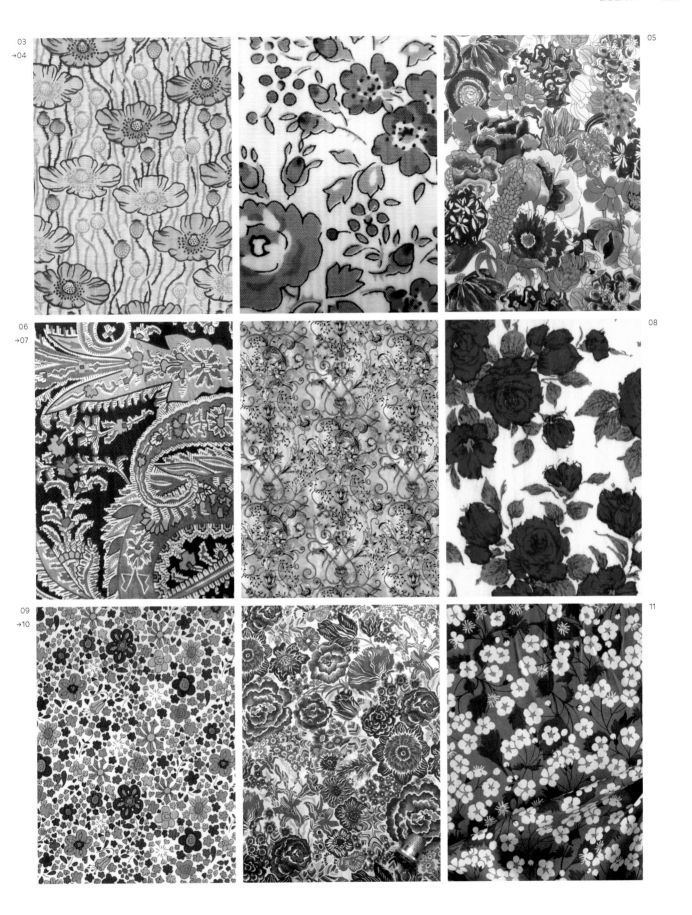

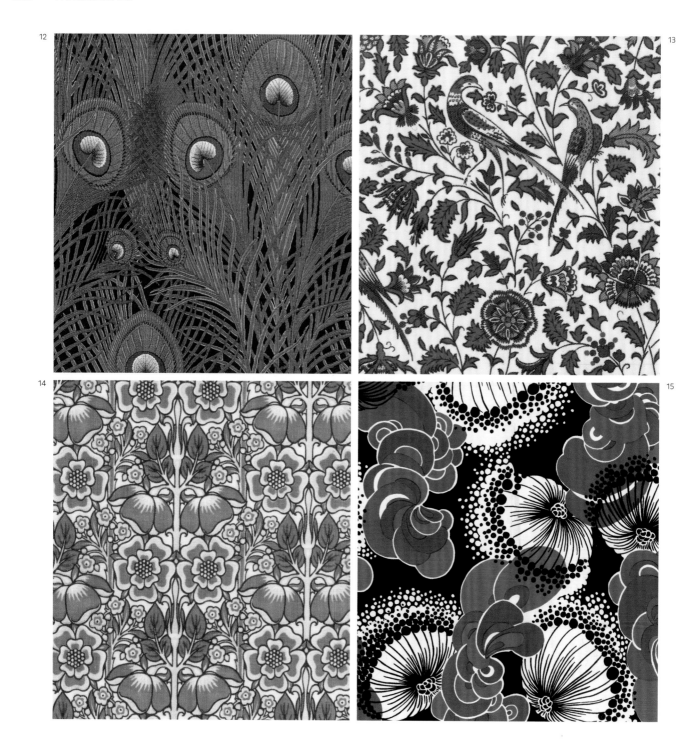

12. 'Hera'/'Peacock Feather', roller-printed cotton. The stylized
peacock-feather motif is long associated with Liberty
(c. 1887).

13. Art Nouveau-inspired print (c. 1906–9).

14. 'Poppyland' fabric printed on cotton (c. 1912–13).

15. 'Seiran' dress fabric, retro print on silk (1960).

16. 'Fundy Bay', graphic abstract landscape, printed
on cotton (1955).

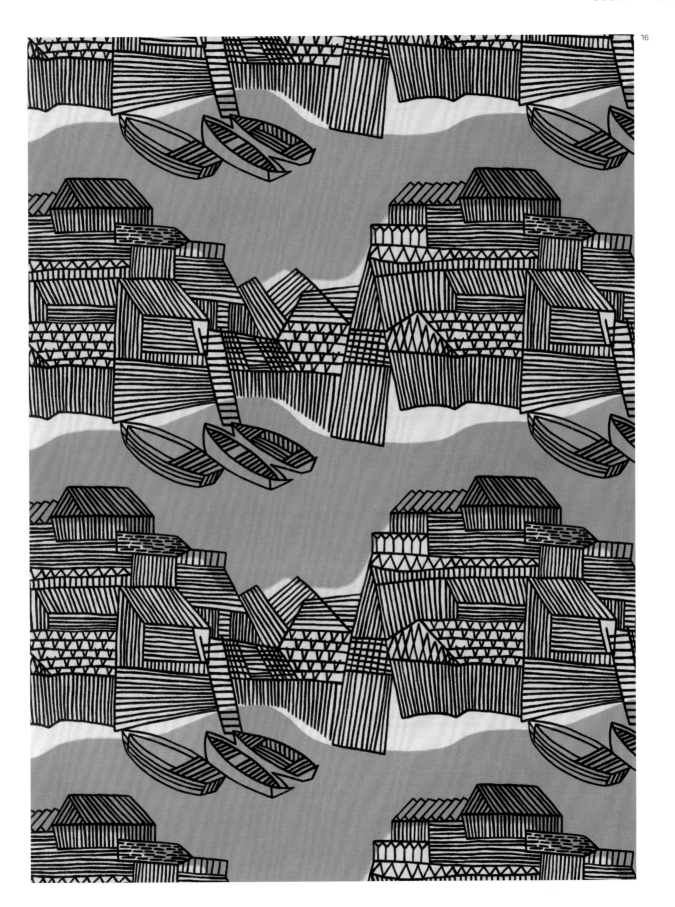

16

LINTON TWEEDS

Forever associated with Chanel's classic bouclé cardigan suit – Linton Mill has provided the French couture house with tweeds since 1928 – Linton Tweeds's high-end cloth can also be seen gracing the catwalks of the biggest labels in fashion, including Oscar de la Renta, Marc Jacobs, Erdem, Rag & Bone, Jaeger and Burberry. In partnership with Cranston Waddell, Scottish-born William Linton opened his mill in 1912 in Carlisle, in northern England. Here he experimented with the traditional rough-hewn tweed in camouflage colours to produce soft lightweight tweeds in a spectrum of dramatic hues suitable for urban wear. Linton Tweeds is now owned by the Walker family and the company produces more than four hundred new designs a year. These tweeds are made in exotic yarns using a vast variety of techniques, although many top fashions houses prefer to rework an existing design from the company's one hundred-year-old archive. Linton Tweeds was awarded the prestigious Queen's Award for Export Achievement in 1991.

COUTURE TWEED

An average Linton tweed might comprise eight different yarns, anything from cashmere, silk, chenille and shirting cotton to Lurex, cellophane or a tufty yarn called Eyelash, in twenty different colours. A couture tweed could contain three hundred different yarns. It can take a day to set up a single loom with the correct rods, piddles, shuttles and shafts for a complex pattern. Oils are used to lubricate the machines, so the tweeds, once they are woven, are expertly washed in huge machines using soft local water.

01. *Textured plain weave in cerise bouclé yarns.*
02. *Textured overcheck of raschel crochet tapes caught into finer weave.*
03. *Interwoven raschel crochet tapes in bouclé yarns on a dark houndstooth ground.*
04. *A pile weave of cut tapes and metallic thread.*
05. *Windowpane grid of slub and bouclé yarns set on canvas-weave ground.*

06. *Multicoloured overlay of floating threads in fancy yarns and tinsel.*

following pages
07. *Large-scale reversible hopsack variant on green houndstooth check.*
08. *Weft-ribbed ground in two colours with slub and tape overcheck and sequins.*
09. *Highly textured houndstooth cloth, with raschel tapes and knitted chainette yarn.*
10. *Houndstooth overcheck in bright tape yarns on coarse hopsack ground.*
11. *Argyle check tweed in bouclé, chiné and metallic yarn.*
12. *Houndstooth check opposing bouclé texture with two-colour tabby-weave areas.*

01
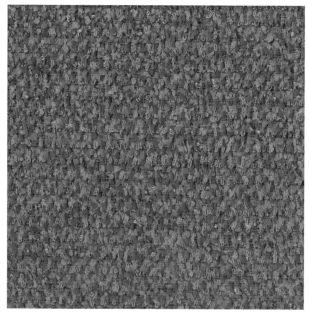

02
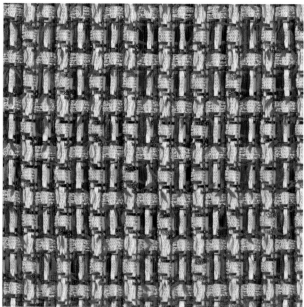

03

04

05

06

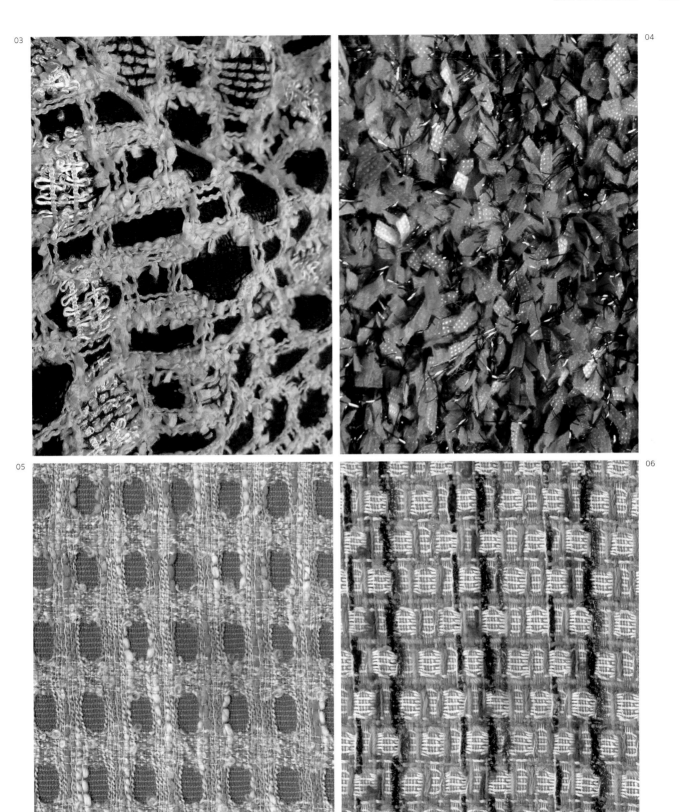

07

08

SPACE-DYEING

Subtle space-dyeing – in which the colour of a yarn is variegated along its length – can be employed to create rich visual texture when used in both warp and weft directions in a cloth. When combined with a structure that also has textural depth and variation in the scale and reflectivity of component yarns, the resultant fabric surface is highly animated.

13. *Houndstooth check variant in vibrant colour relief on white ground.*

14. *Small-scale check from intersecting overcheck yarns.*

15. *Cotton-mix windowpane overcheck in slub and bouclé accent yarns.*

16. *Fancy yarns in an interplay of accent yarn on a melange ground check.*

17. *False plain in rich textures of bouclé and chiné yarns.*

18. *Tonal hopsack weave in fancy textured yarns with flashes of space-dyeing.*

19. *High-relief twill of space-dyed chainette of various sizes on a chiné ground.*

LOUISE GOLDIN

Expert in creating multi-layered pieces to intricate, architectural effect, London-born, New York-based designer Louise Goldin displays a technical virtuosity of painstaking complexity. Having graduated from London's Central Saint Martins College of Arts and Design in 2001 with a BA in fashion knitwear, she later returned to study on the MA knitwear course. Her graduate collection was shown during London Fashion Week in 2005 and was bought exclusively for London store Selfridges. Goldin consolidated her technical and creative expertise as head designer at Brazilian fashion house Tereza Santos for two years and launched her debut collection in London in 2007. The designer also collaborated with Scottish cashmere brand and knitwear manufacturers Ballantyne in 2010 to produce a forty-piece capsule range. Goldin has received a number of awards, including the Fashion Forward prize from the British Fashion Council for brand investment in 2010, the Deutsche Bank Pyramid Award and the Chloé Award.

COMPUTER-AIDED KNITTING TECHNIQUES

Goldin exploits the properties of fine- and heavy-gauge knitted fabrics to fashion futuristic, body-conscious garments and multi-layered pieces by draping and pleating.

01–04. *Colour variations (colourways) of machine-embroidered, knitted double jersey (S/S 2013).*

following pages
05. *Two-colour double jersey jacquard with birdseye backing (S/S 2013).*
06. *Two-colour tubular jersey float jacquard (S/S 2013).*
07. *Peaked effect from increasing and decreasing (S/S 2013).*

01
→02

03

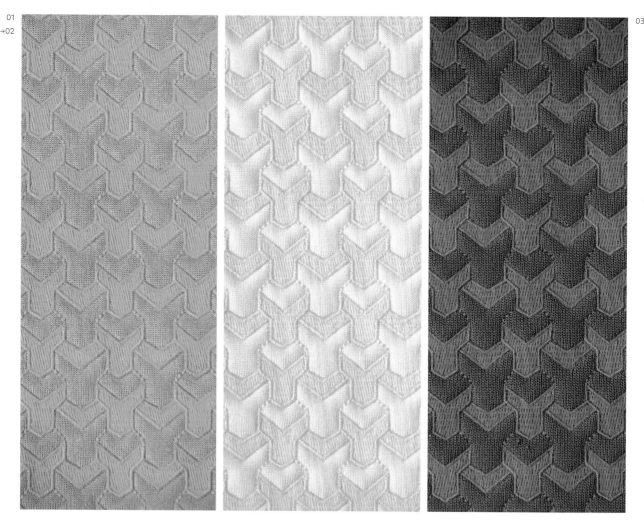

05

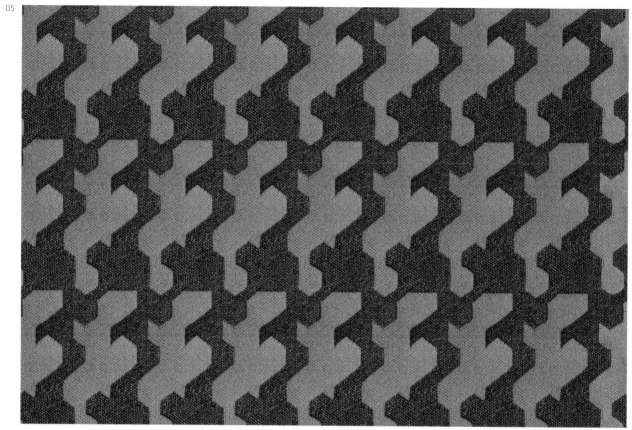

06

LOUISE GRAY

Renowned for the wit and whimsy of her fashion aesthetic, Scottish-born Louise Gray studied at Glasgow School of Art and London's Central Saint Martins College of Arts and Design before founding her eponymous label in 2007. Having successfully shown as part of the Fashion East line-up for the first three seasons, Gray launched her debut solo presentation for Autumn/Winter 2009. Collaborations with ASOS, Brora and Topshop followed, and Gray was a recipient of Topshop/British Fashion Council NEWGEN and Fashion Forward sponsorship. Together with UK accessories label Tatty Devine, Gray created a limited-edition jewelry collection, first seen on the catwalk at her Spring/Summer 2013 show at London Fashion Week. With a bricolage approach to fashion, Gray combines tactility with style.

CRAQUELURE EFFECT
Gray has introduced a craquelure effect by adding a laminated or glossy pigment to the surface of a dark base, seen in swatches **02** and **07**. This is then overprinted with an abstract pattern in green or orange.

01. *Silk screen money print (S/S 2012).*

02. *A screen-printed image is used to produce a craquelure effect (A/W 2013).*

03. *Jacquard weave with text (S/S 2013).*

04. *Jacquard weave with chalkboard graffiti text (A/W 2012).*

05. *Three-colour one-directional vertical jacquard weave (A/W 2013).*

06. *One of a five-piece limited edition for the Smiley Company (S/S 2010).*

following pages

07. *A screen-printed image is used to produce a craquelure effect (A/W 2013).*

08. *Three-colour jacquard weave (A/W 2013).*

01

02
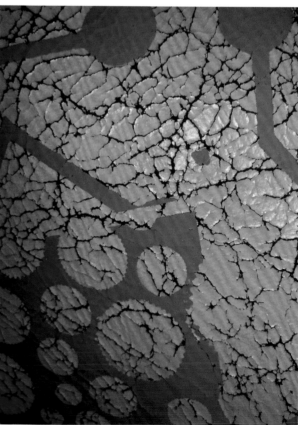

03

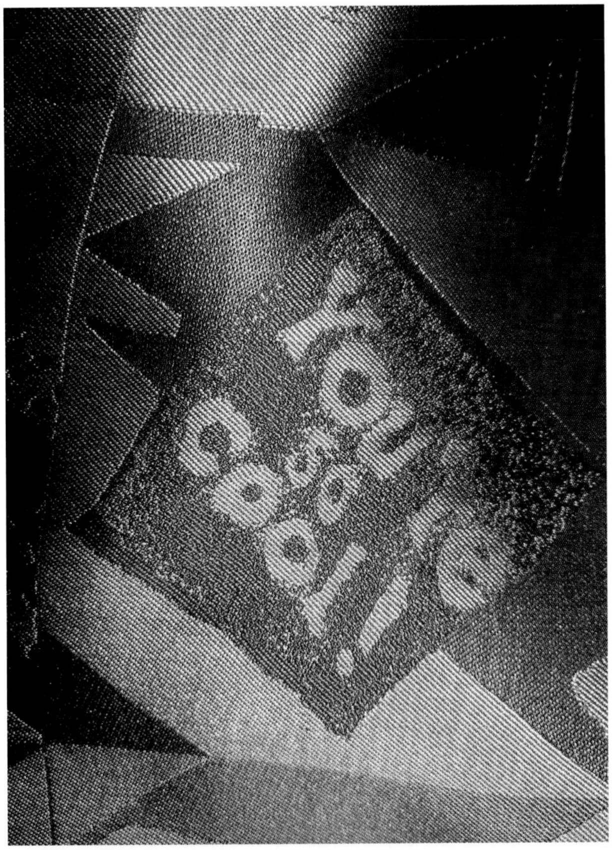

04

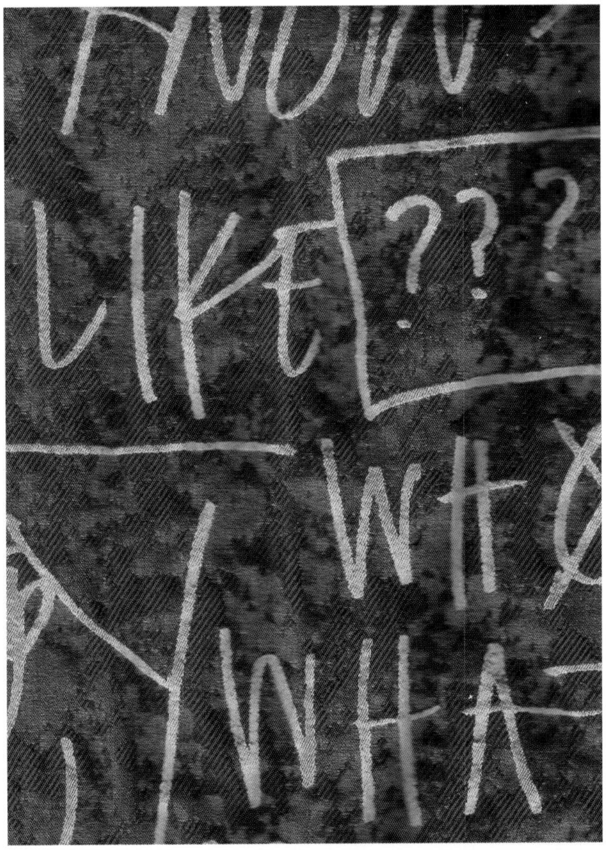

05

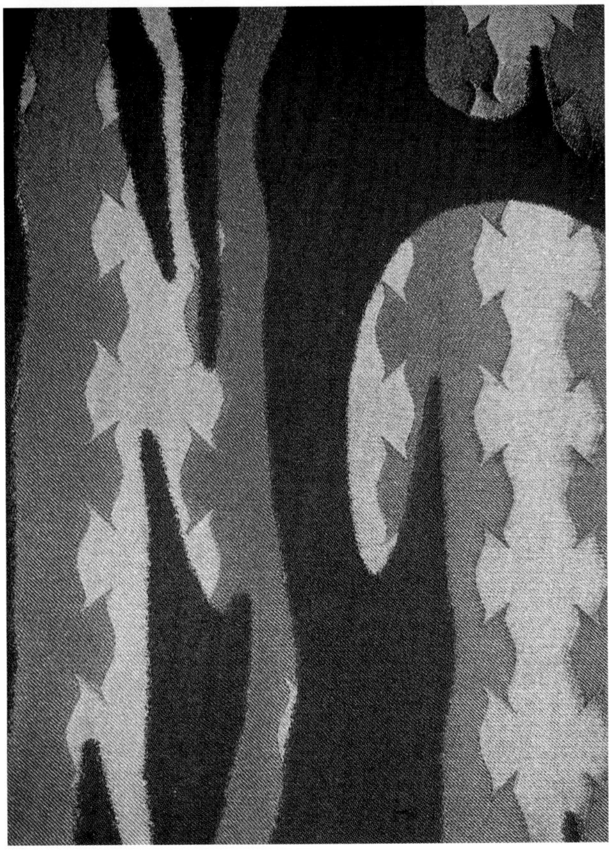

06

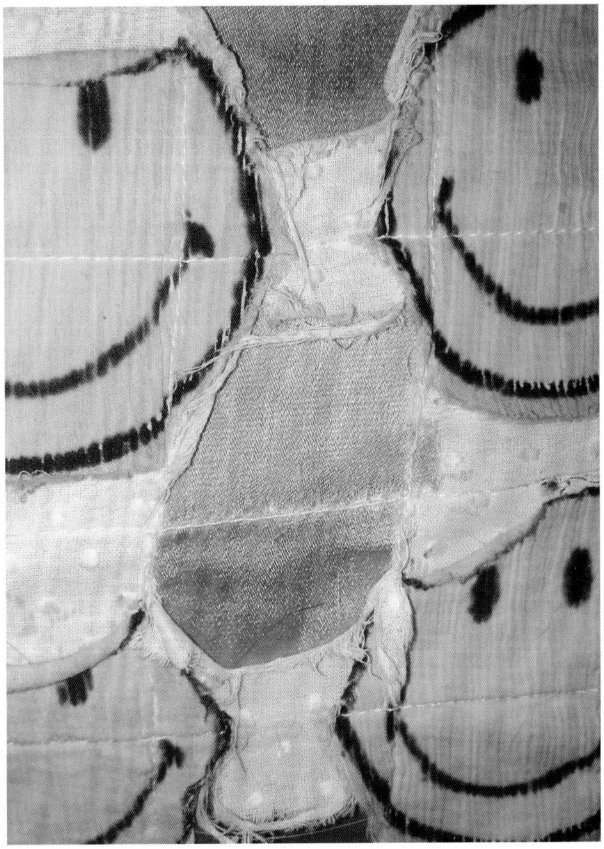

07

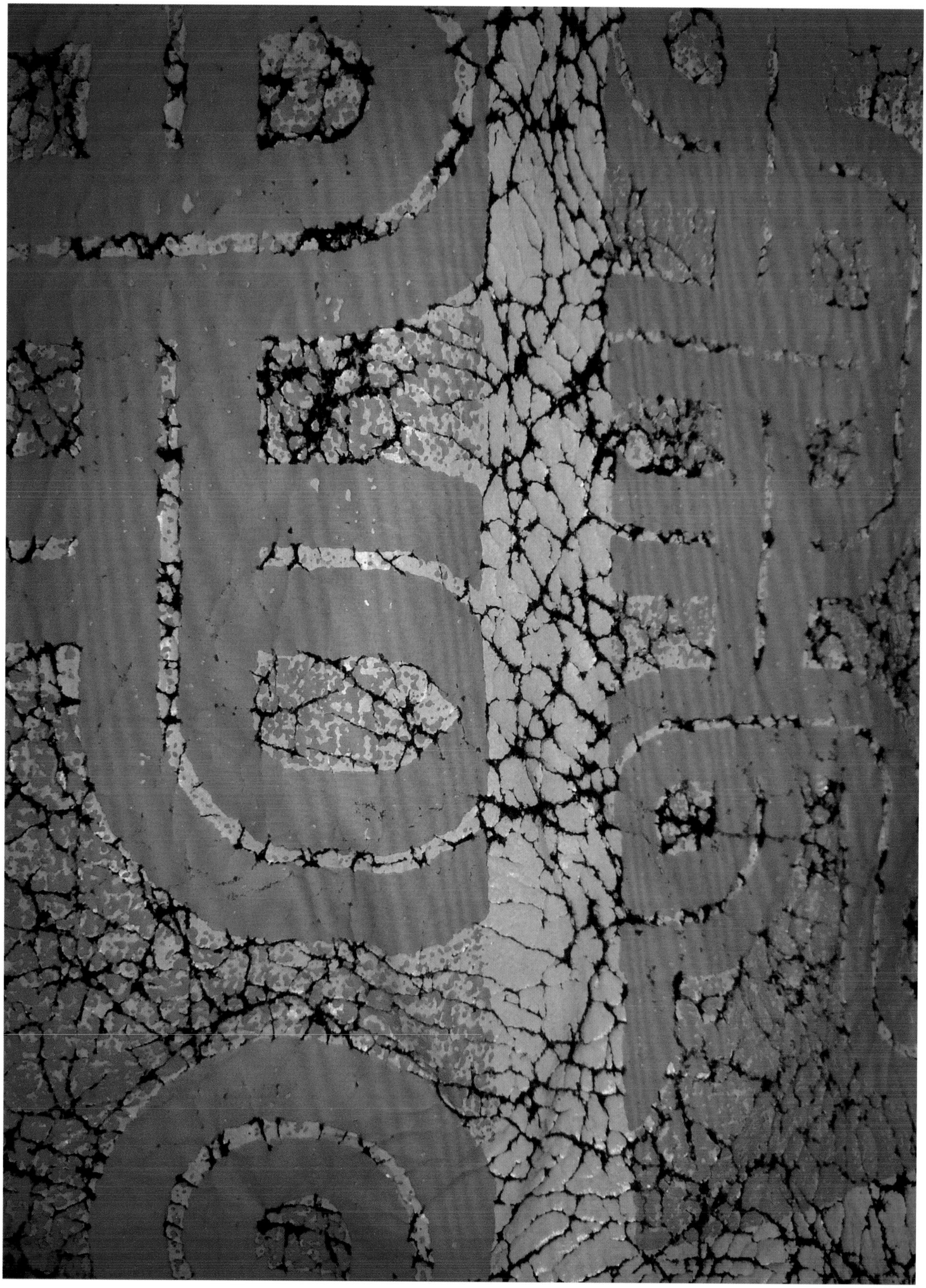

MARIMEKKO

One of the most recognizable and directional fashion and textile brands of the past six decades, Marimekko was founded in 1951 in Finland by visionary textile designer Armi Ratia and her husband, Viljo. The company offered brightly coloured, bold graphic prints of pure abstract form in place of the fussy, small-scale floral motifs then popular in the post-war world. The pioneering artist and freelance designer Maija Isola created 533 designs for the Marimekko

Corporation during the course of her thirty-eight-year career, and to a significant extent the label is still identified with Isola's aesthetic. In 1985, the company was sold to the Amer Group, and subsequently to Kirsti Paakkanen, who introduced new designers to revive the brand. Less fashionable in the 1990s, Marimekko regained popularity in the 21st century with the resurgence of interest in mid-20th-century Scandinavian style.

SCREEN-PRINTING

Marimekko's aesthetic of visual directness and clarity, and its adventurous approach to scale – frequently taking up the full width of the fabric – is reinforced by the processes of abstraction and colour separation inherent in screen-printing.

01. *'Verkko' screen print by Mika Piirainen (1996).*
02. *'Petrooli' screen print by Annika Rimala (1963).*
03. *'Alaris' screen print by Stefan Lindfors (1997).*
04. *'Jäniksen Vuosi' screen print by Aino-Maija Metsola (2008).*
05. *'Räsymatto' screen print by Maija Louekari (2009).*

01

02

03

04

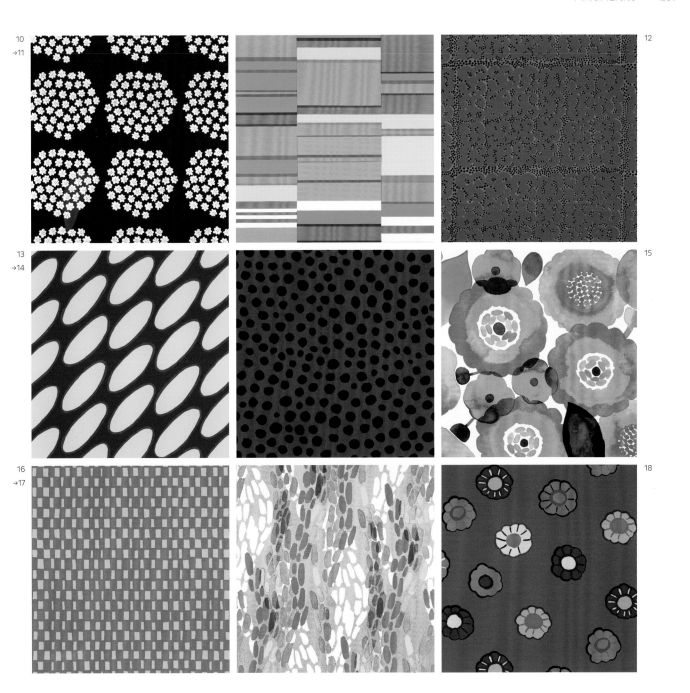

06. *'Acapulco' screen print by Maija Louekari (2008).*
07. *'Dyyni' screen print by Maija Isola and Kristina Leppo (1983).*
08. *'Papajo' screen print by Annika Rimala (1968).*
09. *'Lisko' screen print by Antti Eklund (1994).*
10. *'Puketti' screen print by Annika Rimala (1964).*
11. *'Hyppyraita' screen print by Pentti Rinta (1973).*
12. *'Tarha' screen print by Annika Rimala (1963).*
13. *'Linssi' screen print by Kaarina Kellomäki (1966).*
14. *'Pirput Parput' screen print by Vuokko Eskolin-Nurmesniemi (1958).*

15. *'Kesähelle' screen print by Aino-Maija Metsola (2011).*
16. *'Noppa' screen print by Vuokko Eskolin-Nurmesniemi (1954).*
17. *'Kaarna' screen print by Aino-Maija Metsola (2008).*
18. *'Nekku' screen print by Katsuji Wakisaka (1972).*

following pages
19. *'Pisaroi' screen print by Maija Louekari (2006).*

20
→21

22

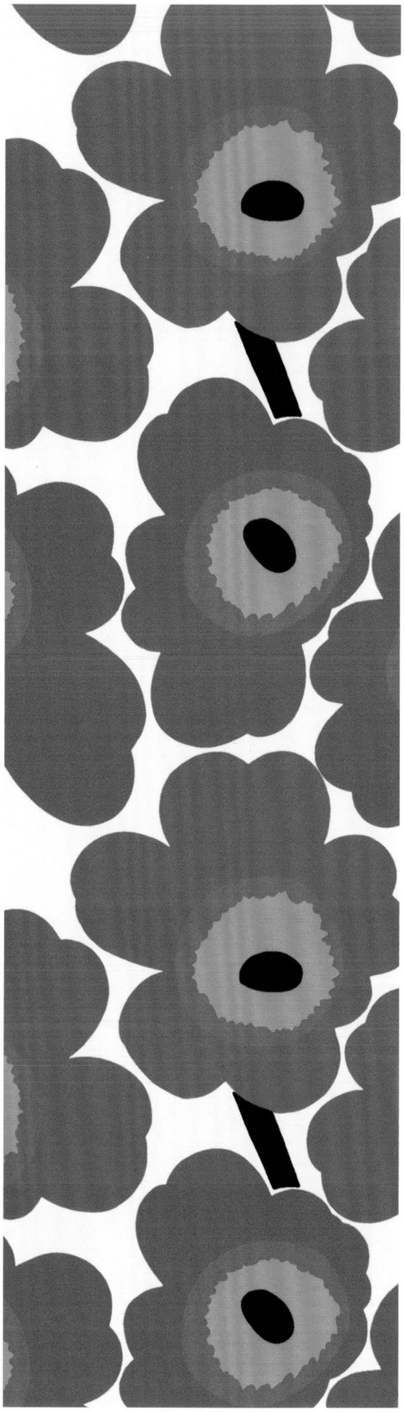

TECHNIQUE

Within a vast output of individual fabric designs, Marimekko has consistently explored the spectrum of abstraction from nature – from geometrics that become organic to floral reductions that convey essences of the source – in arrays that exploit positive and negative space.

20. *'Ryijy' screen print by Maija Louekari (2011).*
21. *'Pikku Suomu' screen print by Annika Rimala (1966).*
22. *'Unikko' screen print by Maija Isola (1964).*
23. *'Lumimarja' screen print by Erja Hirvi (2004).*

MARY KATRANTZOU

Print maximalist Mary Katrantzou was born in Athens and left Greece in 2001 to study architecture at Rhode Island School of Design, USA, before moving to London. Mary Katrantzou's first show-stopping ready-to-wear collection debuted at London Fashion Week in Spring/Summer 2009, with the support of the British Fashion Council and the NEWGEN scheme. Following a trajectory that started after her graduation in 2008 with a collection of only nine dresses and led to worldwide recognition and a slew of awards, including the British Fashion Council Award for Emerging Talent and the Young Designer of the Year at the *Elle* Style Awards in 2012, Katrantzou continues to set the bar with her signature imposition of three-dimensional artefacts. These include Fabergé eggs, perfume bottles and Qing dynasty vases rendered in *trompe l'œil* prints on her sculpted garments.

DIGITAL PRINTING

Katrantzou achieves an intensity of colour, pattern and texture for her thematic collections by means of digital printing. The designs are further embellished with sequins, crystals and three-dimensional appliqué, in keeping with her compulsive exploration of *trompe l'œil* conundrums.

01. *Repetitive swathes of digital flowers (S/S 2012).*
02. *Printed photo-realist gems encrusting a satin base (S/S 2012).*
03. *Loosely mirrored texture print on tussah silk (S/S 2012).*
04. *Crushed cans in* trompe l'œil *print on tussah silk (S/S 2012).*

following pages
05. *Soft focus floral cornucopia (S/S 2012).*
06. *Cut-and-paste montage of hyper-colour marine scene (S/S 2012).*
07. *Shoaling fish intercut digitally with metal artefacts and flowers (S/S 2012).*

pages 266–7
08. *Irises and butterflies float before contoured metal on chapa silk (S/S 2012).*
09. *Whimsical fish, cropped and printed on ripple patterned weave (S/S 2012).*

pages 268–9
10. *Fabric encrusted with crushed cans and a swirl of coloured Swarovski flowers (S/S 2012).*

01
→02

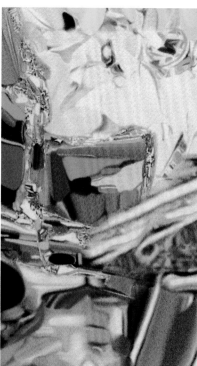
03

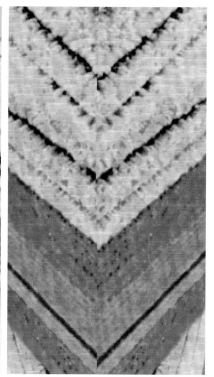

06

07

08

10

MATTHEW WILLIAMSON

With an unerring eye for the juxtaposition of brilliant colour and integrated pattern and embellishment, London-based designer Matthew Williamson first appeared on the fashion scene in 1997 with his acclaimed fourteen-piece graduate collection, 'Electric Angels'. These neon-bright garments of fluid, simple shapes were early evidence of the designer's modern bohemian sensibility, which continued with the launch of his eponymous label in 1997 with business partner Joseph Velosa. Williamson's exuberant luxe-hippie aesthetic

and eclectic use of print were perfectly matched to the Italian label Pucci, where he was the creative director from 2005 to 2008. The designer's signature style has also translated successfully to the high street, with a long-running diffusion line, 'Butterfly', for British department store Debenhams introduced in 2002 and a high-profile co-branding exercise with Swedish company H&M. The award-winning Matthew Williamson flagship store on Bruton Street, Mayfair, opened in 2004.

USE OF COLOUR

The effect of Williamson's renowned use of saturated colour is generally heightened by the inclusion of black graphic elements incorporated into the design of the prints. These are rendered in rich embroidery and brocades.

01. *'Mosaic Spirograph' (A/W 2009).*
02. *'Desert Floral'. Shada kaftan print exclusive for online retailer Net-A-Porter (S/S 2008).*
03. *'Leopard Peacock' (S/S 2004).*
04. *'Tiger Lace' (A/W 2007).*
05. *'Rainbow Leopard' (RTW A/W 2007).*
06. *Signature peacock-feather print (S/S 2004).*

01

02

07

08

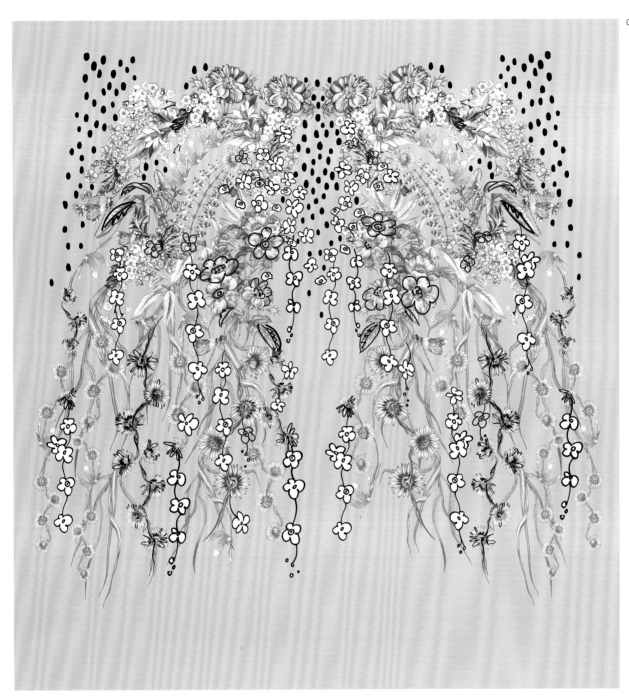

this page
07. *'Dragonfly Graffiti' (S/S 2014).*
08. *'Imperial Burst' (A/W 2012).*
09. *'Wild Botanical' (S/S 2014).*

following pages
10. *Pixelated floral print (S/S 2013).*
11. *'Cactus Garden'. One-directional cactus print (Resort 2014).*

10

12

this page
12. 'Precious Rose' (A/W 2013).
13. Chintz-like peony print (A/W 2006).
14. 'Waterlilies' (S/S 2007).
15. 'Marble Flower'. Chinoiserie-inspired floral print (A/W 2005).
16. 'Orchid Scatter' (S/S 2010).

following pages
17. 'Imperial Eagle' (A/W 2012).
18. 'Blossom Faze' (S/S 2012).
19. 'Starburst'. Agitated kaleidoscopic florals (S/S 2009).
20. 'Kerala Spice'. Landscape print (S/S 2013).
21. 'Sunburst Ink'. Motion-blurred spectrum placement print (S/S 2013).

17

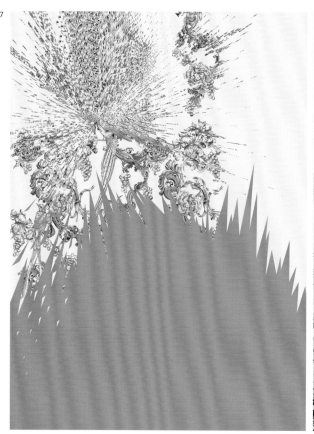

18

19

20

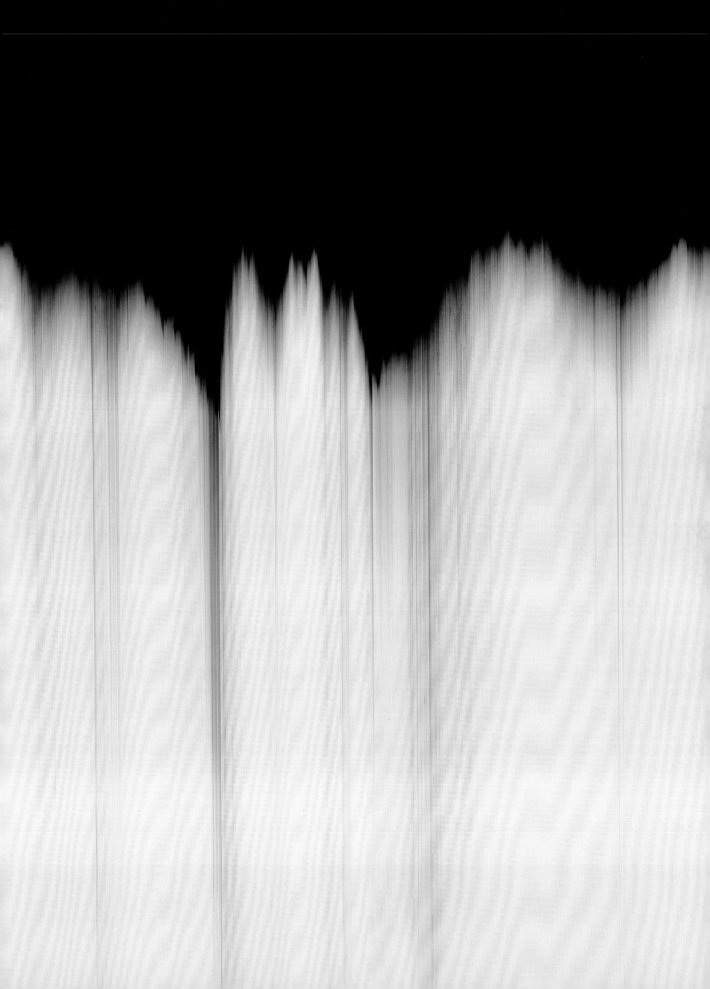

this page

22. *Peacock feather on chiffon in chain stitch and bugle bead embroidery (S/S 1998).*

23. *Beaded cut-out ikat embroidery on crêpe georgette (S/S 2012).*

24. *Maharaja mirror beading on embroidered bustier dress (S/S 2013).*

25. *Peacock-feather chiffon weave, encrusted with couched fibre bundles and sequin chains (S/S 2011).*

26. *Fringed macramé bustier in multi-strand embroidery floss (S/S 2011).*

27. *Ndebele-style banded beading, forming a halter bodice (S/S 2008).*

28. *Bodice with maharaja mirror and metal bead embroidery, bordered by satin cords on double jersey (S/S 2013).*

29. *Baroque encrusted panel of quartz and glass beads, layered with metallic paillettes and feather fronds (S/S 2012).*

following pages

30. *Heavy banded bodice, embroidered in wood and metal beads, with crystals, chains and faceted studs (S/S 2011).*

31. *Tiered layers of pleated chiffon, interspersed with bands of chain-stitched tulle and metal plate paillettes (S/S 2011).*

32. *Chiffon-weave skirt panel embroidered with a cascade of couched sequin and bundled fibre chains, tasselled with bugle beads (S/S 2011).*

28

29

30

31

MEGAN PARK

Renowned for the artisanal quality of her hand-dyed and embellished textiles, Australian designer Megan Park spends three months of every year in India overseeing the development of her simply structured, meticulously French-seamed garments. Park designed for Givenchy, Dries Van Noten and Kenzo in London, before finally launching her own label in 1997 with an eponymous collection of evening bags and scarves. Having established her reputation internationally, in 2004 she returned to Australia, where she and her team are based. Every intricately embroidered Megan Park fabric is designed in-house, striking a balance between traditional Indian craftsmanship and contemporary aesthetics. Park's inspiration often comes from her archive of vintage and antique textiles.

DIGITAL PRINTING

These all-over multi-directional digital prints revisit the vocabulary of floral textiles, retaining the core symbolism of florid reference in complex and refreshing impressionistic concoctions. Images of stylized flora – sourced from embroidery or watercolour renditions – are captured, digitally filtered and recoloured before being layered and intercut into flowing swathes of pattern, texture and colour.

01. *Layered digital print bricolage (2011).*
02. *Digital montage of impressionistic florals (2011).*
03. *Washed and torn paper digitally captured and montaged (2011).*
04. *Multi-layer foliar digital composite (2011).*
05. *Japanese-inspired layered floral assemblage (2011).*

01

02

03

04

06

07

08

09

10

TAMBOUR BEADING

Megan Park works with a team of artisans in New Delhi
to incorporate a variety of different beads, sequins, crystals
and stones into her designs using tambour-beading techniques
(known in India as *arhi* or *zardozi* embroidery).

06. *Resist-dyed indigo cloth (2012).*

07. *Metallic tambour embroidery with paillettes (2012).*

08. *Floral spray in bugle beads and sequins (2012).*

09. *Covered paillettes and chain-stitched jersey (2012).*

10. *Floral roundels in geometric plastic flats (2012).*

MICHAEL VAN DER HAM

Netherlands-born designer Michael van der Ham first showed at London Fashion Week in 2011, exhibiting his arresting technique of juxtaposing various prints and weights and textures of cloth in one garment, including devoré, crushed velvet, embroidery, and jacquard weave and knit. The designer worked as an intern at Sophia Kokosalaki and at Alexander McQueen before studying for a master's degree in fashion at Central Saint Martins College of Arts and Design in London, from which he graduated in 2007. Van der Ham was the recipient of the British Fashion Council NEWGEN catwalk sponsorship for London Fashion Week for Spring/Summer 2012. He was also one of three emerging London-based fashion names chosen to create costumes for the Opening Ceremony of the London Olympics in 2012. In the same year, the designer collaborated with Scottish cashmere label Brora for a capsule knitwear collection.

FAUX PATCHWORK PRINT
Developing his initial theme, Michael van der Ham collages together various torn swatches in multicoloured engineered prints on crêpe de Chine. The result is a faux patchwork of multiple graphic images rendering a two-dimensional surface in three dimensions.

01. *Detail of faux patchwork, printed on crêpe de Chine (S/S 2012).*
02. *Fragments of faux shibori technique as part of patchwork print (S/S 2012).*

following pages
03. *Collaged print (S/S 2012).*
04. *Collaged print (S/S 2012).*
05. *Collaged print (S/S 2012).*
06. *Collaged print (S/S 2012).*

01

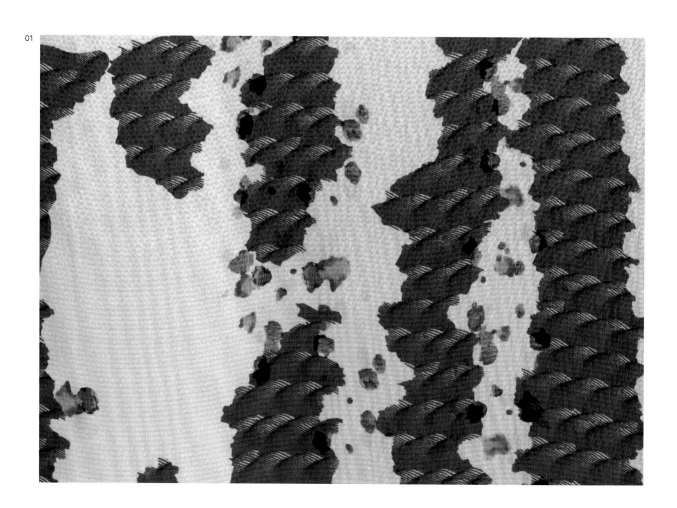

03

04

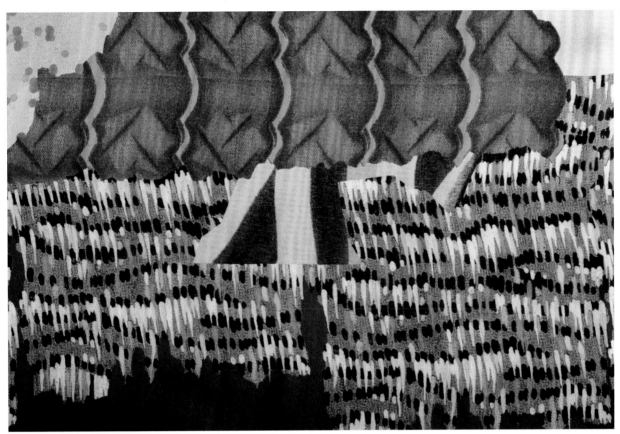

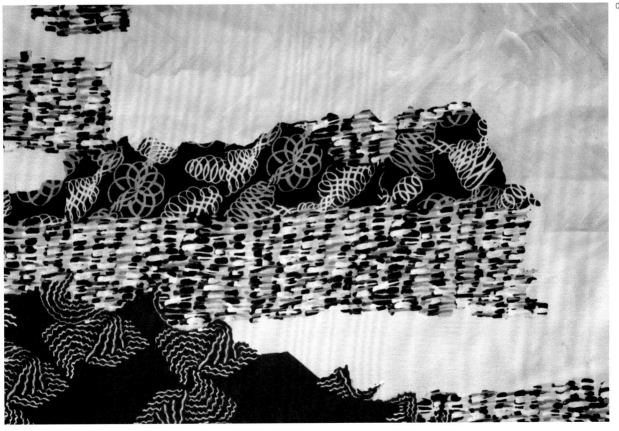

07
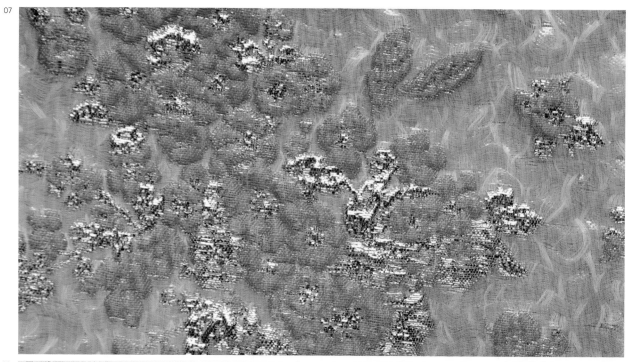

08
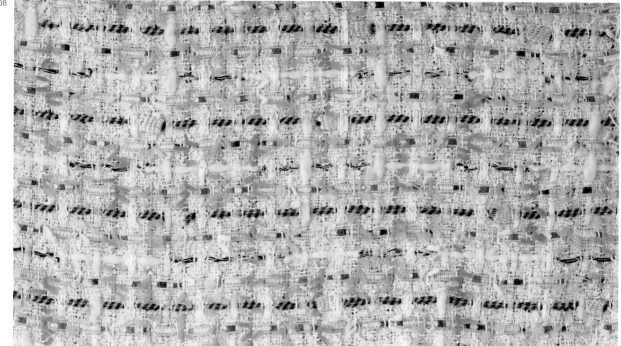

HAND DOBBY WEAVING

Michael van der Ham utilizes the qualities of dobby weaving
to combine an irregular white warp and weft with a
secondary insertion of fancy yarns fabricated from strips
of various cloths, thereby producing a rich surface with
an artisan appearance.

07. *Laminated metallic jacquard weave (S/S 2012).*
08. *Fringed hand-weave (S/S 2012).*
09. *Metallic jacquard jersey knit (A/W 2011).*

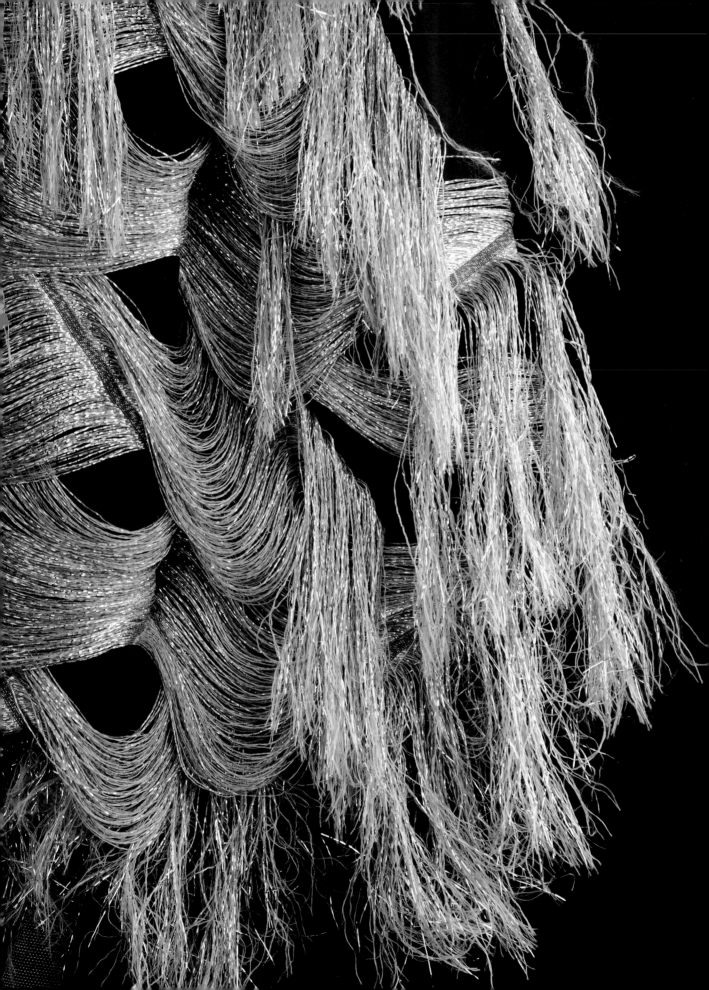

NUNO CORPORATION

With a family heritage of traditional Japanese textile manufacture, Junichi Arai had already established himself as a significant inventor in his field by 1966, with intellectual property rights granted to him in relation to thirty-six separate textile processes. His research and development drew further on the textiles of other cultures, such as those of Central America, which led to a characteristic hybridization of both inspiration and technology. During the 1970s and 1980s, Japanese fashion design was closely associated with Arai's fabrics and made a global impact. Consequently, in 1984, the designer opened the original Nuno store in Tokyo, together with Reiko Sudo. Nuno simply means 'cloth', and it is a succinct expression of the label's design philosophy of quiet eloquence.

TECHNICAL INNOVATION

Distinguished by a technical and aesthetic eclecticism, Nuno cloths have been gathered into museum study collections around the world. Gifted with detail, each cloth has a bespoke prescription that sustains impact from close forensic examination and from the perspective of a complete artefact.

01. *'Tsunagi'. Chips of Nuno remnants, hand-stitched to dissolving fabric (2004).*
02. *'Streaks And Steps'. Woven with kibiso, the outer silk of the cocoon shell (2008).*
03. *'Contour Line'. Using fibres that dissolve to an opalescent gossamer (1987).*

01

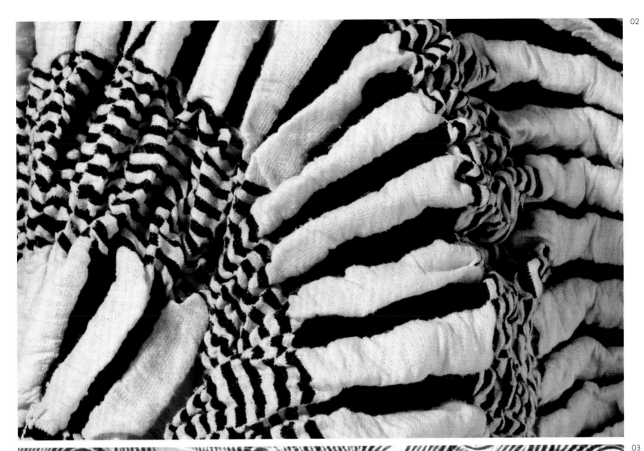

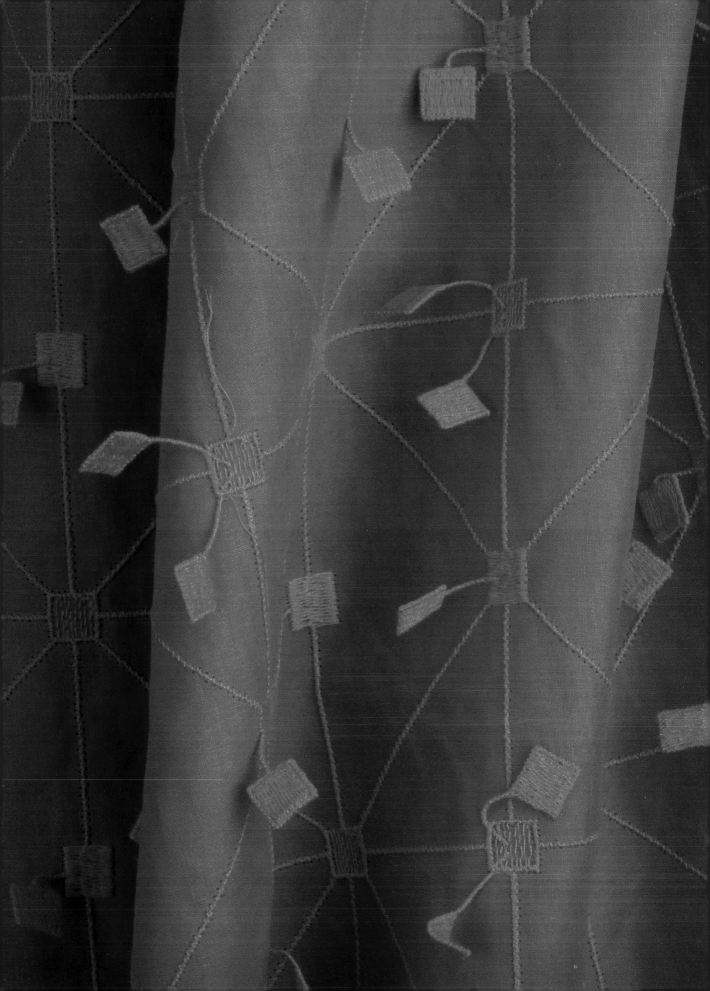

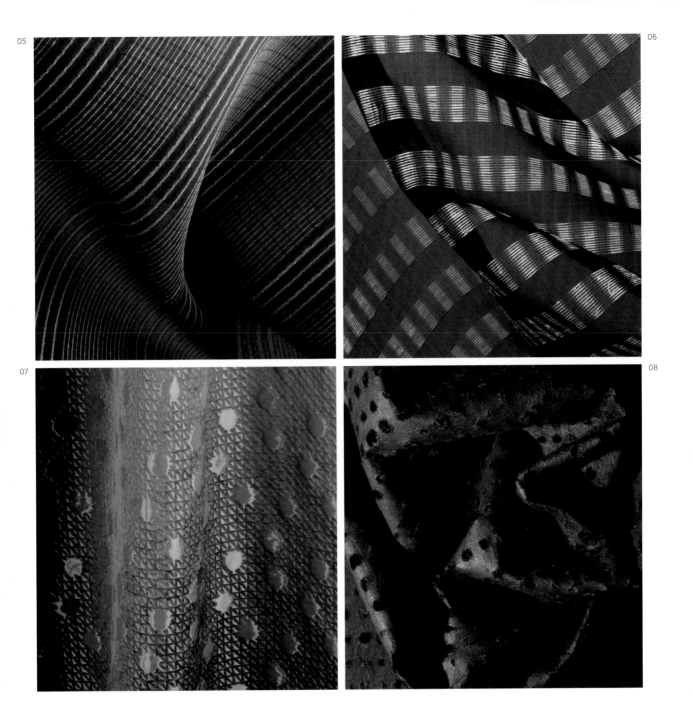

05

06

07

08

CONTROLLED RHYTHM

The patterning in Nuno cloths – even within false plains –
exhibits a controlled variegation of rhythm, as in the music
of the traditional Japanese stringed instrument the *koto*,
in which small excursions from predictable tempos animate
the general flow.

04. *'Swinging Squares'. Embroidered with freely swinging
squares (2008).*

05. *'Suzushi Stripe'. Designed by Reiko Sudo in raw silk and
kibiso (2009).*

06. *'Itomaki Kibiso'. Designed by Reiko Sudo in silk (2009).*

07. *'Satin Snow'. High-gloss satin jacquard quilted brocade
(2005).*

08. *'Amate'. Polyester and rayon with paper, named after
a Mexican bark cloth (2000).*

HYBRID TECHNOLOGIES

Within the lexicon of visual attributes explored by Nuno, texture in opposition to the insubstantial or the transparent is obsessively addressed, with innumerable incarnations across an array of hybrid technologies. The interaction or illusion of positive and negative spaces is held in balance to lead the eye through and beyond the unit of repeat.

previous pages
09. *'Polygami'. Pleated polyester weave, emulating patented origami pleats (2009).*

this page
10. *'Stalactite'. Shutter series by Kazuhiro Ueno in polyester stitched tape (2007).*
11. *'Paper Roll'. Designed by Reiko Sudo, nylon tape strips stitched onto a soluble base (2002).*
12. *'Basketweave'. Sheer woven cloth, concertina shrunk with thermoplastic (2006).*

10

11

PAUL SMITH

Britain's most commercially successful designer, Paul Smith built his initial reputation on 'classics with a twist' menswear, offering traditional tailoring but with idiosyncratic detailing. He opened his first shop in his home town of Nottingham in 1970, and he became the first retailer to make Covent Garden a shopping destination when he opened his first London store there in 1979. By popular demand Smith was persuaded to launch a womenswear range in 1993, and these collections continue to convey the designer's quintessentially English aesthetic of juxtaposing formality with quirkiness, with the emphasis on vibrant prints. In 1998 Smith introduced the concept of the curated shopping experience when he opened his premises on Kensington Park Road in Notting Hill, London. The designer was honoured with a knighthood in 2001 for his services to the fashion industry.

FOULARD

A foulard is a lightweight twill or plain-woven silk weave printed with a small-scale, multi-directional pattern with basic block repeat in various colours. Although usually reserved for scarves and neckties, Paul Smith appropriates the design for men's and women's outerwear.

01. *Foulard design with spot repeat (S/S 2012).*
02. *Polka dot foulard design (S/S 2012).*
03. *Foulard design in block repeat (S/S 2012).*
04. *All-over digital print of fishing flies (S/S 21012).*
05. *Digital photo-realist all-over print of roses (S/S 2012).*

01
→02

03

04

05

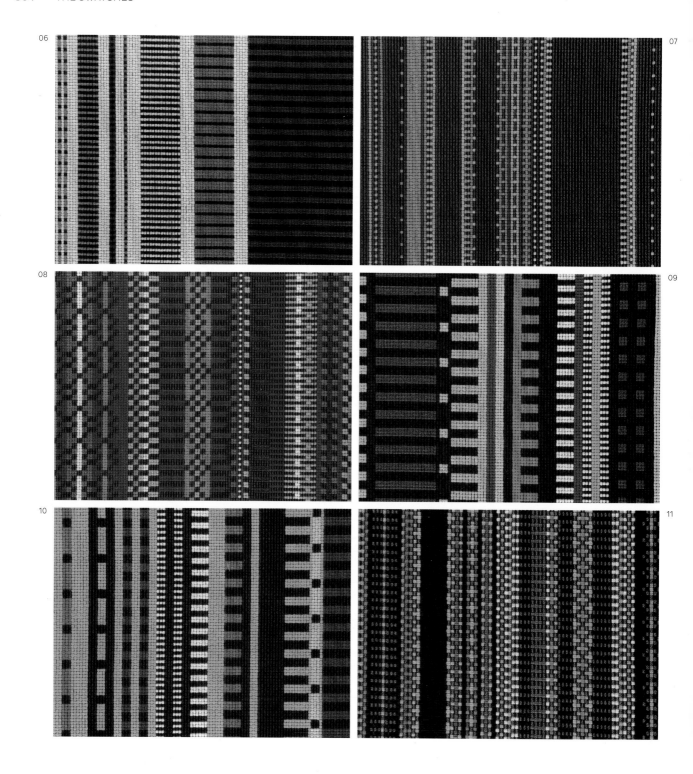

JACQUARD WEAVE

Faux tapestry weave, commonly known simply as tapestry weave, is woven on a loom that has a jacquard 'harness' attachment to control individual warps. This gives the appearance of a tapestry weave that is normally made by an intensive hand-worked embroidery process.

06–11. *Polychromatic striped cloth in a series of colours that progresses through the spectrum of faux tapestry weave in various combinations and scales (S/S 2012).*

12. *Digital all-over print featuring breeds of dog in a complex half-drop repeat (S/S 2012).*

PAUL VOGEL

Founder of one of the first independent design studios to use CAD textile systems, British-born Paul Vogel specializes in woven design with an emphasis on yarn-dyed checks and stripes. With a client list that includes Ralph Lauren, Calvin Klein, Abercrombie & Fitch, Stussy, Kate Spade, Aubin & Wills, Jack Wills and Etro, Vogel established his Clerkenwell design practice in 1991 after spending two years with one of Italy's leading textile designers, Cecchi Lido, designing fabrics for Benetton, Emporio Armani and Jean Paul Gaultier. The textile design studio exhibits at most major trade shows, including Première Vision Paris and New York, with seasonal collections shown to a variety of international clients. Vogel also works on specific design projects directly with his clients and mills. The designer is a visiting lecturer at Nottingham Trent University, the Royal College of Art, and Central Saint Martins College of Arts and Design in London.

APSO DOBBY WEAVE PROGRAM
Paul Vogel uses the Apso dobby weave computer program to design his fabrics. This allows the designer to manipulate all the elements of a woven fabric accurately, simulating the fabrics on screen and offering a perfect reproduction of pattern and colour.

01. *Yarn-dye shirt in 100% cotton for Jack Wills (A/W 2009).*
02. *Yarn-dye shirt in 100% cotton for Aubin & Wills (A/W 2009).*
03. *Yarn-dye shirt in 100% cotton for Stussy (S/S 2002).*
04. *Yarn-dye shirt in 100% cotton for Aubin & Wills (A/W 2009).*
05. *Scarf in 100% cotton (S/S 2010).*

06. *Yarn-dye shirt in 100% cotton for Aubin & Wills (A/W 2009).*
07. *Yarn-dye shirt in 100% cotton for Aubin & Wills (A/W 2009).*
08. *Yarn-dye shirt in 100% cotton for Aubin & Wills (A/W 2009).*
09. *Yarn-dye shirt in 100% cotton for Aubin & Wills (A/W 2009).*

following pages
10. *Yarn-dye shirt in 100% cotton for Stussy (S/S 2002).*
11. *Yarn-dye shirt in 100% cotton for Jack Wills (A/W 2012).*
12. *Yarn-dye shirt in 100% cotton for Jack Wills (A/W 2012).*
13. *Yarn-dye shirt in 100% cotton for Stussy (S/S 2002).*
14. *Yarn-dye shirt in 100% cotton for Aubin & Wills (A/W 2011).*

01
→02

03

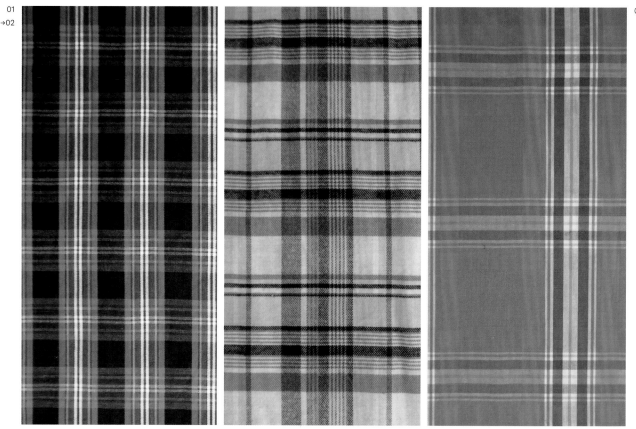

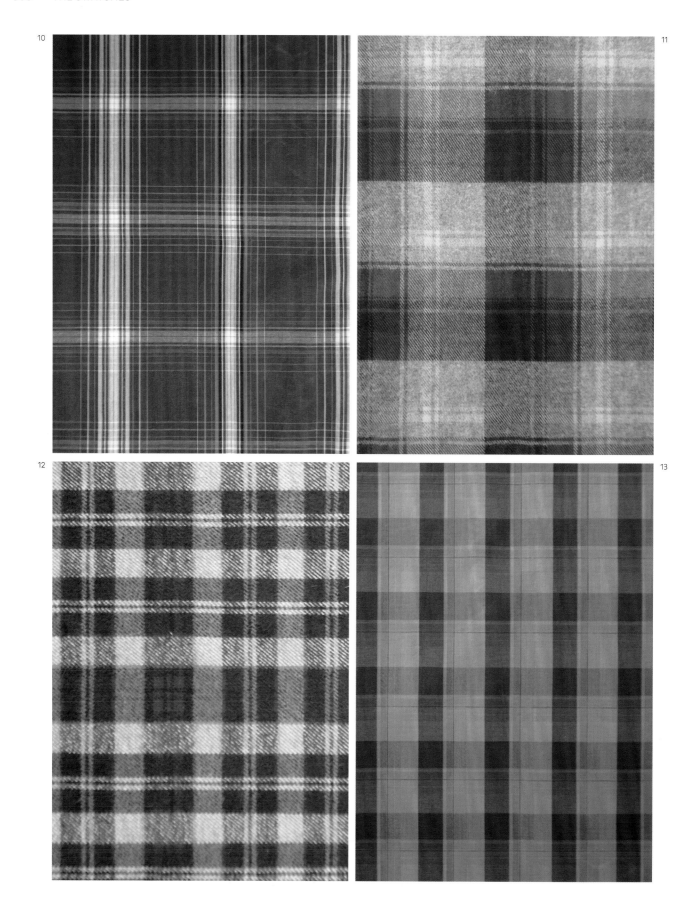

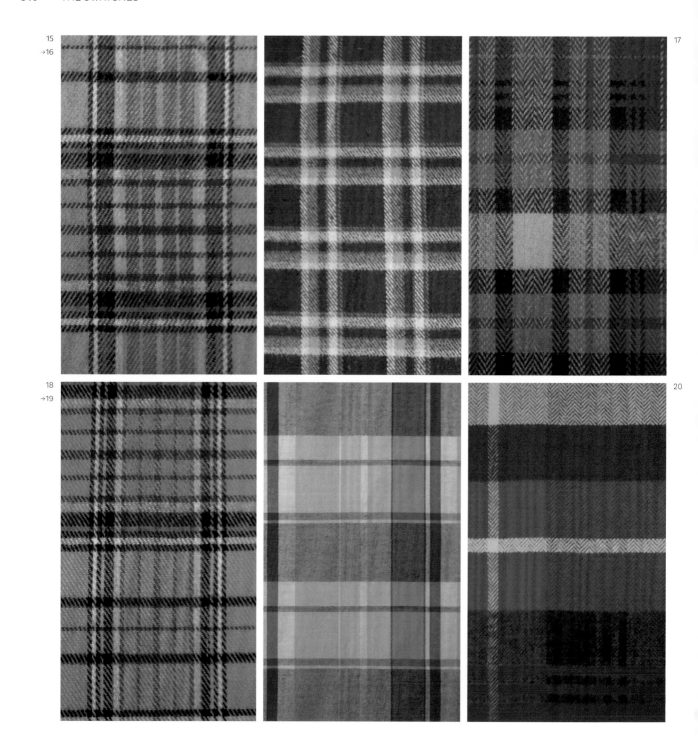

15. *Scarf in 100% lambswool for Avoca (A/W 2012).*
16. *Yarn-dye shirt in 100% cotton for Aubin & Wills (A/W 2011).*
17. *Scarf in 100% cashmere for Avoca (A/W 2012).*
18. *Scarf in 100% lambswool for Avoca (A/W 2012).*
19. *Yarn-dye shirt in 100% cotton for Aubin & Wills (S/S 2010).*
20. *Scarf in 100% lambswool for Avoca (A/W 2012).*
21. *Yarn-dye shirt in 100% cotton for Jack Wills (Christmas 2010).*

PETER JENSEN

Danish designer Peter Jensen utilizes an extensive visual vocabulary, often inspired by idiosyncratic source material and references to popular culture. He also works in collaboration with various artists and photographers. In 2009 Jensen designed a capsule collection for an installation with British fashion photographer Tim Walker, before going on to create a highly acclaimed collection in 2010 based on his collaboration with US artist and photographer Laurie Simmons. Jensen's work with brands has included projects with Topshop, Topman, Fred Perry, Weekday, Urban Outfitters and B Store. His wide-ranging influences stem from his early training in graphic design, embroidery and tailoring. In addition to appearing regularly at London Fashion Week, Jensen's designs are stocked in a variety of prestigious stores and boutiques in more than twenty countries on five continents. He is currently head of menswear on the MA course at Central Saint Martins College of Arts and Design in London.

DIGITAL PRINTING

Digital printing makes it possible to transfer a picture directly from a digital camera or computer screen to cloth using unlimited colours; it is therefore ideal for a designer such as Jensen whose work is often image-led. The image can be adjusted within seconds, be it to rescale, recolour or reconfigure the design.

01. *'London Print' from the* Muriel *collection (A/W 2010).*
02. *'Trees And Trains' from the* Fanny *collection (A/W 2005).*

following pages
03. *'Soldier Print' from the* Muriel *collection (A/W 2010).*

01

04

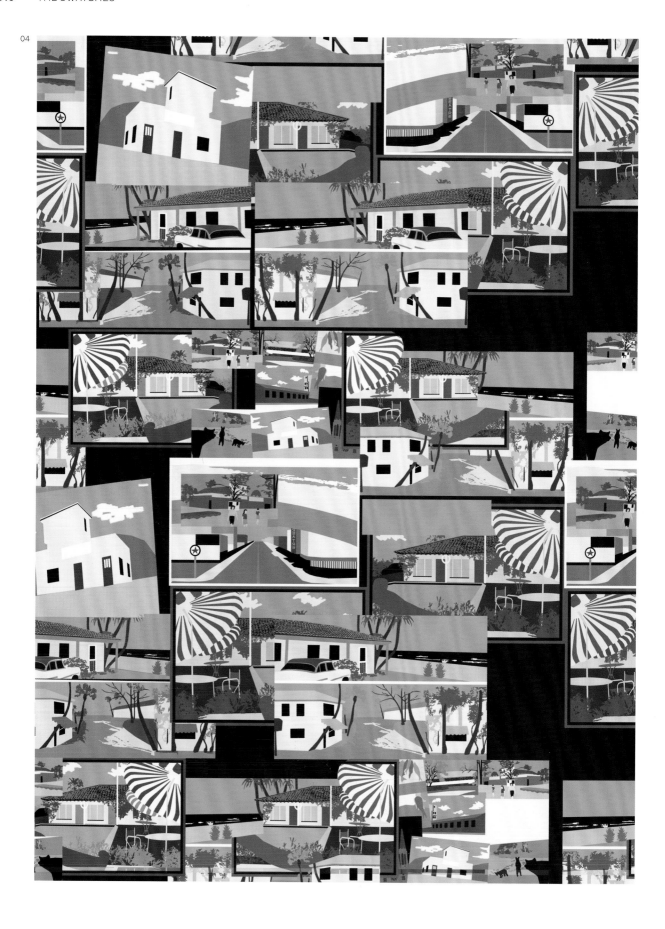

CONVERSATIONAL PRINTS

Many of Peter Jensen's prints exploit the ease with which digital montage can be used to construct complex scenic microcosms that engage the eye with detail and humour, both in colour and in monochrome.

04. *'Postcards' from the* Meryl *collection (Resort 2012).*
05. *'Doghead' from the* Jytte *collection (A/W 2009).*
06. *'Carpet Print' from the* Laurie *collection (S/S 2010).*
07. *'Jazz Club' from the* Nina *collection (S/S 2012).*
08. *'Rabbit Woodblock' from the* Nina *collection (S/S 2012).*

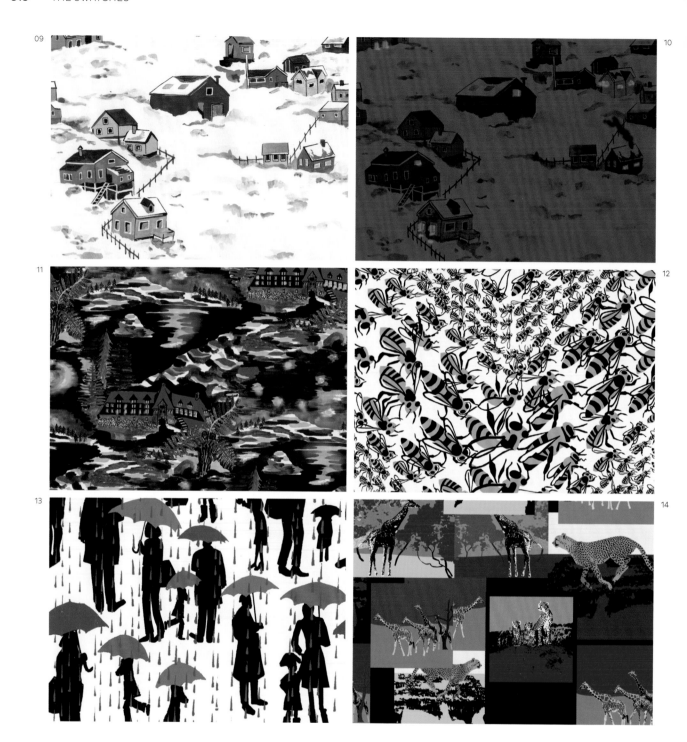

ALL-OVER STEP AND REPEAT MOTIFS

The rapid duplication and rotation of isolated stylized or
figurative motifs in Peter Jensen's prints create rhythmic
arrays of all-over pattern in classic step and repeat manner.

09. *'Greenland Day'* from the Jytte *collection (A/W 2009).*

10. *'Greenland Night'* from the Jytte *collection (A/W 2009).*

11. *'Oregon Scenic'* from the Shelley *collection (S/S 2011).*

12. *'Diagonal Wasp'* from the Shelley *collection (S/S 2011).*

13. *'Umbrella'* from the Anna-Karina *collection (A/W 2011).*

14. *'Safari'* from the Nina *collection (S/S 2012).*

15. *'Frames'* from the Gertrude *collection (S/S 2004).*

PREEN BY THORNTON BREGAZZI

Founded in the mid-1990s, the independent British label Preen, now known as Preen by Thornton Bregazzi, has evolved from a small shop selling recycled vintage items in London's Portobello Road Market to a globally recognized brand. The couple behind the label, Justin Thornton and Thea Bregazzi, purvey a vintage-influenced aesthetic of classic silhouettes, although it was a cult body-conscious power dress resonant of the 1980s from their Spring/Summer 2007 collection that initially drew them to the attention of the international fashion press. Preen first showed at London Fashion Week in 2000 and moved to New York in 2008, before returning to show in London in 2013. The designers have produced high street collaborations for British retailer Debenhams and a diffusion range, Preen Line.

PIXELATION

Digital printing is deployed by the label to introduce a pixelated print of traditional floral motifs. Pixelation occurs where the resolution of an image or a portion of an image is lowered to deliberately introduce a blurred outline with serrated edges.

01. *Photographic digital print of flowers (S/S 2013).*
02. *Pixelated digital print (S/S 2012).*

following pages
03. *Placement print for yoke and hem (S/S 2012).*
04. *Colour-blocked digital print (S/S 2012).*

01

03

04

SILKEN FAVOURS

With a witty and idiosyncratic approach to textile design, Victoria Murdoch, the creative talent behind the label Silken Favours, produces hand-drawn illustrative prints for the luxury scarf market. A former model, Murdoch went on to study textile design at Chelsea College of Art and Design in London, graduating with first-class honours. The designer uses traditional, complex and labour-intensive pen-and-ink techniques for her illustrations, which include playful and whimsical juxtapositions of subject matter, finding much of her inspiration in the natural world. Silken Favours has been stocked exclusively at Liberty of London, where the company's first range of silk scarves was launched in July 2011. Since then the designer has had her own window display at Liberty and extended her range to include bespoke cushions and a collection of clothing that features playsuits and shirts.

HAND ILLUSTRATION
All the prints are hand-drawn and then scanned into a computer. Colour is applied before the design is digitally printed onto silk.

01. *'Scottish Splendour' from the* British Beasties *collection (2012).*
02. *'Quintessentially English' from the* British Beasties *collection (2012).*
03. *'Puppy Passion' from the* Heart *collection (2011).*
04. *'Elegant Equines' from the* Heart *collection (2011).*
05. *'Amphibian Amours' from the* Heart *collection (2011).*
06. *'Butterflies And Beasties' from the* Heart *collection (2011).*
07. *'I Love Everything' from the* Heart *collection (2011).*
08. *'Succulent Strawberries' from the* Heart *collection (2011).*

01

02

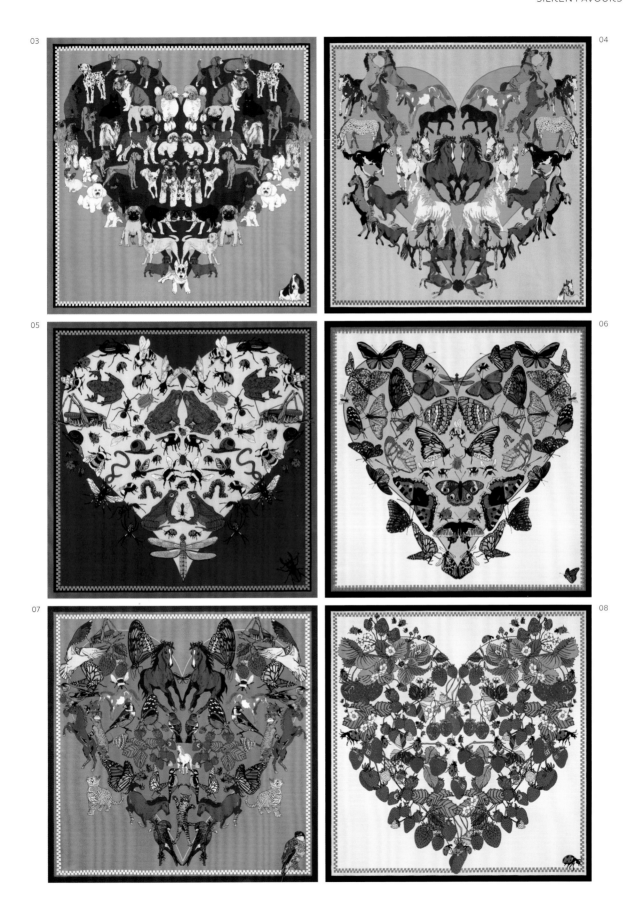

09

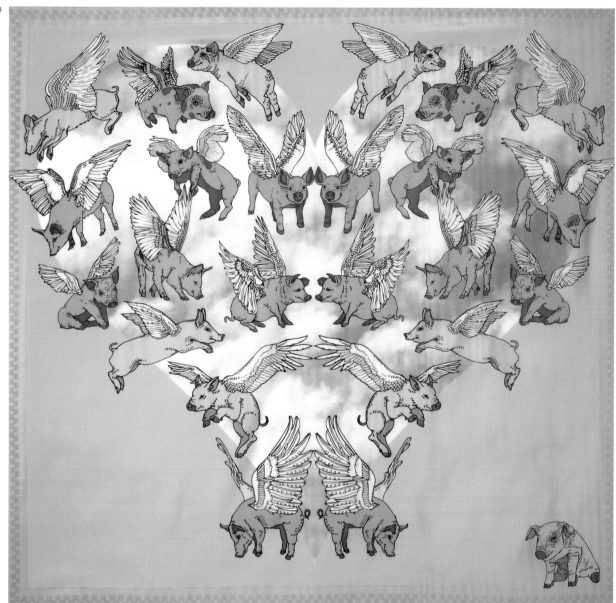

09. *'Psychedelic Swine' from the* Animal Fantasy *collection
(2012).*

10. *'Precious Pussies' from the* Animal Fantasy *collection (2011).*

11. *'Intricately Irish' from the* British Beasties *collection (2012).*

12. *'Wonderfully Welsh' from the* British Beasties *collection (2012).*

13. *'Trippy Kitty' from the* Animal Fantasy *collection (2012).*

14. *'Kaleidoscopic Crustaceans' from the* Animal Fantasy
collection (2012).

15. *'Bounteous Birds' from the* Heart *collection (2012).*

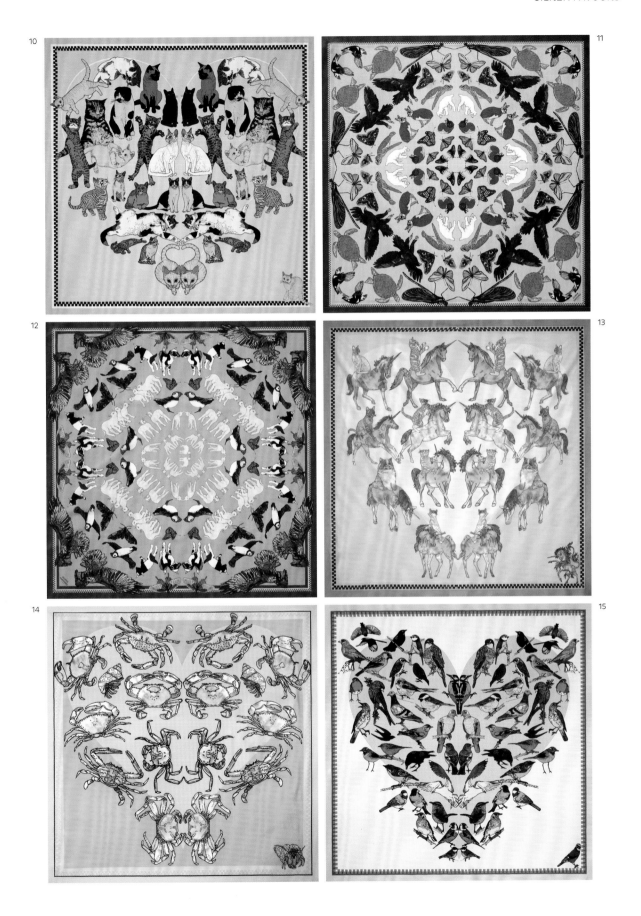

SONIA RYKIEL

Once described as the 'queen of knitwear' by the New York fashion press, French fashion legend Sonia Rykiel opened her first boutique in 1968 on Paris's Left Bank at the height of the youthquake movement. The label's signature style of colourful stripy knits on black, cardigan dresses and *trompe l'œil* effects later included elements of deconstruction, with unhemmed edges and reversed seams. Rykiel diversified into lifestyle products in 1976; fragrances, childrenswear, menswear and shoes followed. The second line, Inscription

Rykiel (renamed Sonia by Sonia Rykiel in 1999), was created in 1989 and the main line's flagship store opened on Boulevard Saint-Germain the following year. In 2008, a show at the national park of Saint-Cloud celebrated the fortieth anniversary of the house. In 2012, Sonia Rykiel received two French honours: the Great Vermeil Medal of the City of Paris and the insignia of Commander of the Order of Arts and Letters; a year later she was promoted to the prestigious rank of Grand Officer of the National Order of Merit.

TACHIST PRINT

From the French word *tache* meaning 'a stain, spot or blot', a tachist mark is one in which the brush and paint is allowed free reign over the surface of the material (**04** and **05**).

01. *Details from a digital print on silk (A/W 2008).*
02. *Details from a digital print on silk (A/W 2008).*
03. *Details from a digital print on silk (A/W 2008).*

following pages
04. *Tachist-effect print on textured ground (S/S 2013).*
05. *Reverse image, tachist-effect print on textured ground (S/S 2013).*

01

02

03

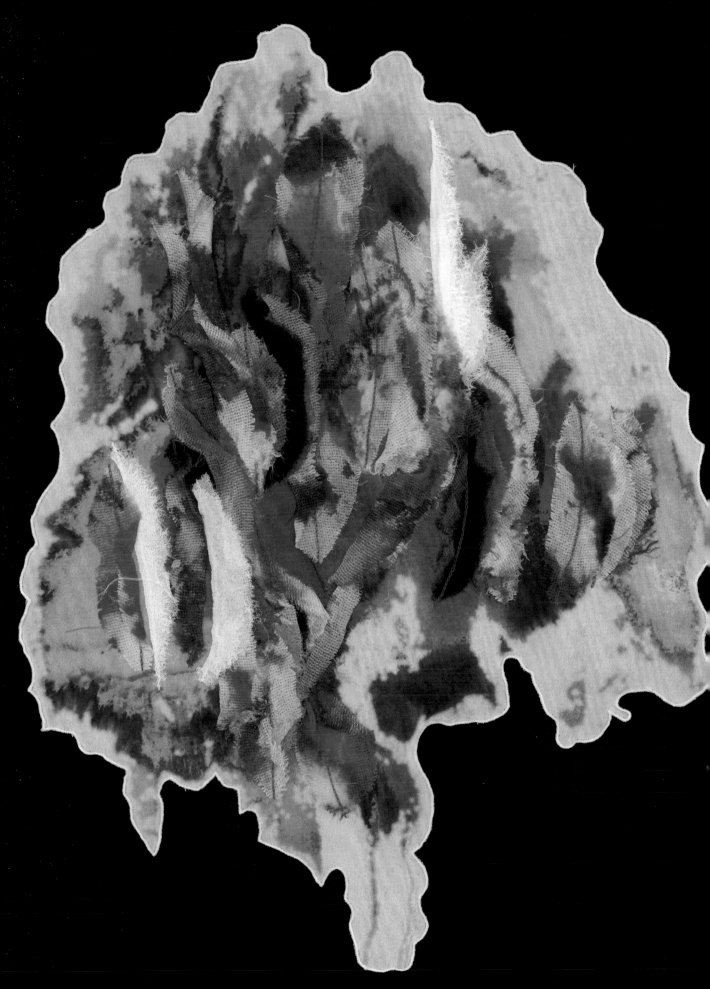

06

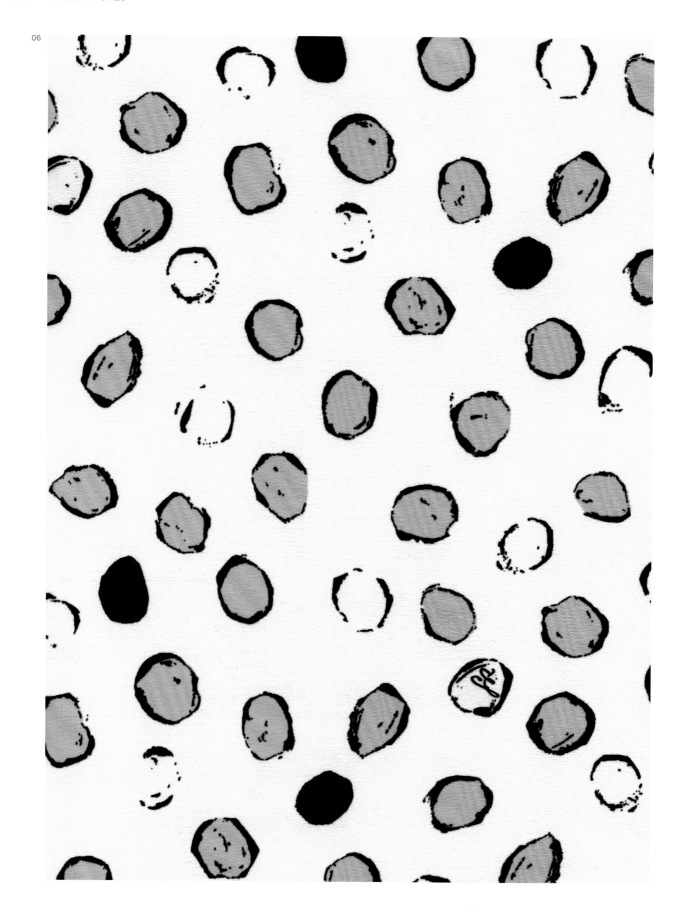

07

08

09

10

11

12

13

14
→15

16

previous pages
06. *Spot repeat print (S/S 2011).*
07. *One-directional floral print (S/S 2012).*
08. *Diffused tulip motifs (S/S 2012).*
09. *Logoed multi-directional print (S/S 2011).*
10. *Photo-realist print (S/S 2012).*

this page
11. *Layered print over a discharge base (A/W 2013).*
12. *Layered print under a discharge base (A/W 2013).*
13. *Layered print over a discharge base (A/W 2013).*
14. *Embroidery with metallic jewelry (A/W 2013).*
15. *Appliquéd bows in a half-drop repeat (A/W 2013).*
16. *Beading over warp-knit base (A/W 2013).*

SOPHIA KOKOSALAKI

Never straying far from her Greek roots, Athens-born Sophia Kokosalaki made her debut at London Fashion Week in 1999, and in 2002 she was appointed chief designer of costumes for the 2004 Olympic Games opening and closing ceremonies in Athens. She is renowned for the skilful draping and ruching of her chiffon goddess dresses, which made her the obvious choice to head the newly resurrected fashion house Vionnet for two years from 2006. Kokosalaki has also designed for Black Gold, a denim and leather label owned by Diesel, and she presented her collections twice a year on the catwalk in New York from 2009 to 2012. Later ventures include the development of a capsule wedding gown line for online retailer Net-A-Porter in 2012 and the launch of Kore Sophia Kokosalaki. This lower priced collection features lace handmade by Sri Lankans as part of an ASOS programme that helps designers to develop alternative revenue streams.

EMBOSSED LEATHER

Tooling, stamping and embossing are terms that refer to the craft of impressing three-dimensional images onto leather (**01**). It is a process that confers both colour and texture to the surface of the skin.

01. *Hand-tooled embossed leather (A/W 2000).*
02. *Coarse hand-knit from patterned knitted braid (A/W 2001).*
03. *Leather and tarnished metal (A/W 2009).*
04. *Leather and tarnished metal (A/W 2009).*
05. *Metallic embroidery (A/W 2010).*

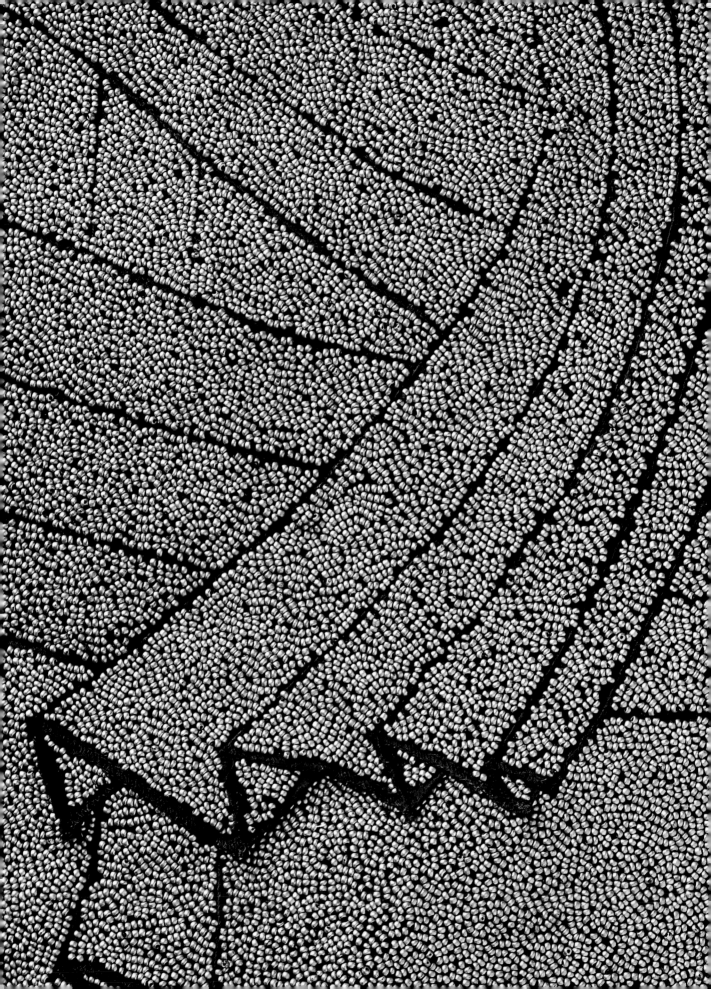

07

08

09

10

11

12

CORDED PINTUCKS

Corded pintucking is achieved by placing cotton yarn
or thread below the cloth in the centre of the pintuck.
Kokosalaki creates corded pintucks that form a convoluted
swirling pattern (**08**).

06. *Illusory drapery in metallic rocaille beads on leather
(S/S 2009).*

07. *Quilted silk satin (S/S 2007).*

08. *Curved corded pintucks (S/S 2007).*

09. *Pearl beads on leather (S/S 2010).*

10. *Densely stitched accordion pleated print (A/W 2000).*

11. *Layered and embroidered tulle (S/S 2010).*

12. *Reverse embossed leather (A/W 2009).*

SOPHIE HALLETTE

Sophie Hallette is the world's premier lace manufacturer, with a renowned client list that includes Valentino, Elie Saab, Christian Dior and Alexander McQueen – creative head Sarah Burton chose the company to make the lace for Catherine Middleton's wedding dress on her marriage to Prince William in 2011. The firm has remained a family business in Caudry, France, since it was founded by Eugène Hallette in 1887.

MACHINE-MADE LEAVERS LACE

The firm uses one hundred-year-old British looms, built in Nottingham, to weave the lace and recreate its handmade qualities. Around thirty new laces are introduced each season and the company has a rolling collection of over two thousand designs. It takes an average of seven years to train a lacemaker.

In 1942 tulle maker Etienne Lescroart bought the company and it has remained in his family for three generations. The design heritage of the company was enriched in 1998 by the acquisition of Riechers Marescot, whose archives provide additional patterns each season. In the 21st century, this delicate, expensive textile is continually reworked for modern tastes, as witnessed in its enduring popularity on the catwalk.

01. *Chantilly lace with floral pattern on a net background embellished with smocking.*
02. *Leavers lace hand embroidered with hand-crafted (Loro Piana) cashmere cords.*
03. *Iconic Leavers flower-pattern lace from the Riechers Marescot collection (early 20th century).*

01
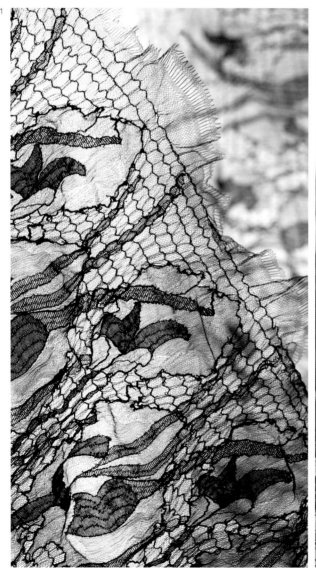

02

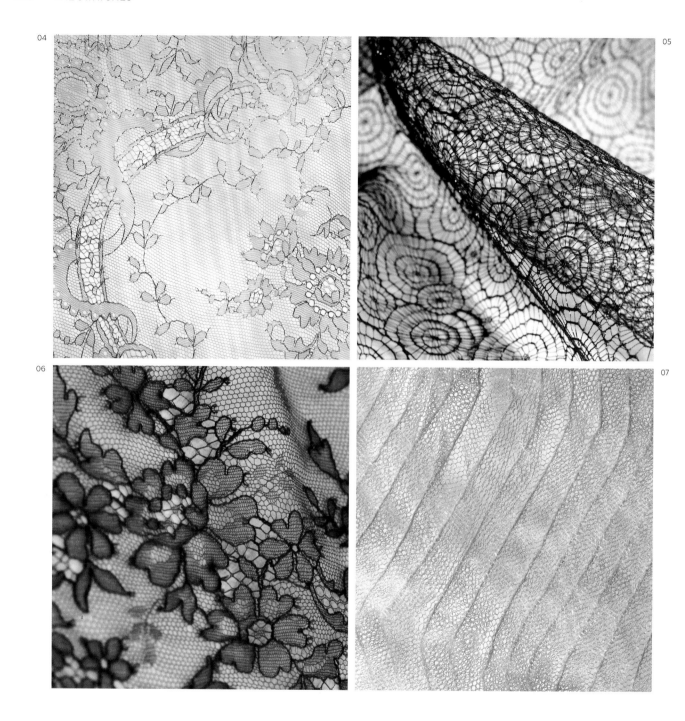

04 | **05**

06 | **07**

LACE MANUFACTURING

The production of machine lace is remarkably complex because it aspires to represent fabrics that were constructed, historically, by labour-intensive manual techniques. Bobbinet looms were the precursors of the famous Leavers lace machines, which remain the technology that most closely is able to reproduce hand bobbin lace of various traditions.

04. *Leavers lace with a classical, romantic flower pattern on a fine mesh of metallic yarn.*

05. *Geometric pattern, Riechers Marescot collection (c. 1930).*

06. *Chantilly Leavers lace with iconic lace pattern (1962).*

07. *Bobbinet tulle in 100% silk. Designed with a hand embroidery technique in a wave pattern.*

08. *Chantilly Leavers flower pattern lace with a delicate hand-scalloped border.*

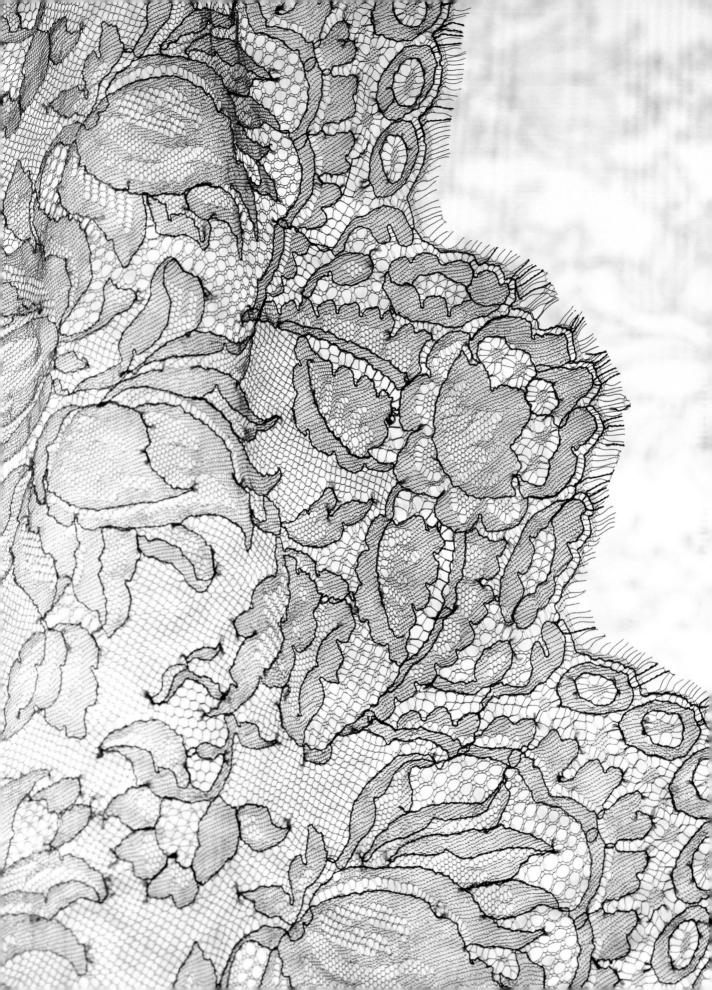

STEPHEN WALTERS AND SONS*

With its origins in the silk weaving district of London's Spitalfields in the 17th century, Stephen Walters and Sons has remained a family-owned business since Benjamin Walters completed his apprenticeship and worked as a weaver in Paternoster Row. In 1860, the company moved to its current premises in Sudbury, Suffolk, where it continues to prosper. A long association with royalty has included special commissions for ceremonial occasions such as the robe and coach for the coronation of Queen Elizabeth II in 1953 and the wedding dress for Lady Diana Spencer in 1981. Stephen Walters and Sons has a large historical archive and extensive reference studio. Now under the aegis of Julius Walters, from the ninth generation of the family, the company produces six new collections each year, in addition to bespoke projects. All design and production takes place in-house at the mill in Suffolk.

STEPHEN WALTERS AND SONS FOR DIOR

TECHNIQUE

The company creates four seasonal collections each year for neckwear fabrics. In order to ensure that ties fall elegantly and knots sit in smooth forms, ties are cut on the bias (diagonally) across the cloth. For this reason, designs are generally drafted for legibility 'on the cross'. Tie fabric is commonly made of extremely fine yarn with more than ninety 'ends' per centimetre.

01. *Micro-jacquard with weft floats in geometrically patterned strips (mid-1990s).*

02. *Alternate colourway of swatch (**01**). The black warp is constant (mid-1990s).*

03. *Micro-jacquard, giving an illusion of receding steps when cut on the bias (mid-1990s).*

04. *To sustain the illusion of depth, two-tonal weft colours float across the fixed black warp (mid-1990s).*

05. *Close tones reduce the illusory depth to subtle texturing (mid-1990s).*

following pages

06. *Bengal stripe in repp silk, a tight woven weft ribbed cloth (mid-1990s).*

07. *College stripe in black-and-white repp silk (mid-1990s).*

08. *Regimental stripe in repp silk, disrupted by a tonal suffusion and change of scale (mid-1990s).*

09. *Shadow twill pinstripe on satin silk (mid-1990s).*

10. *Awning stripe in vibrant silk faille (mid-1990s).*

11. *Blazer stripe in repp silk (mid-1990s).*

01
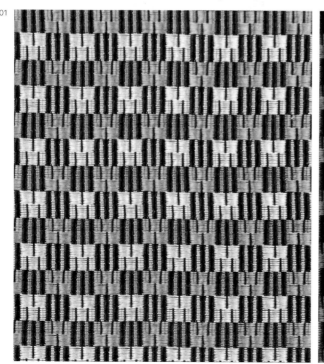

02
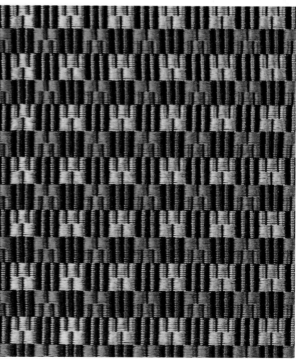

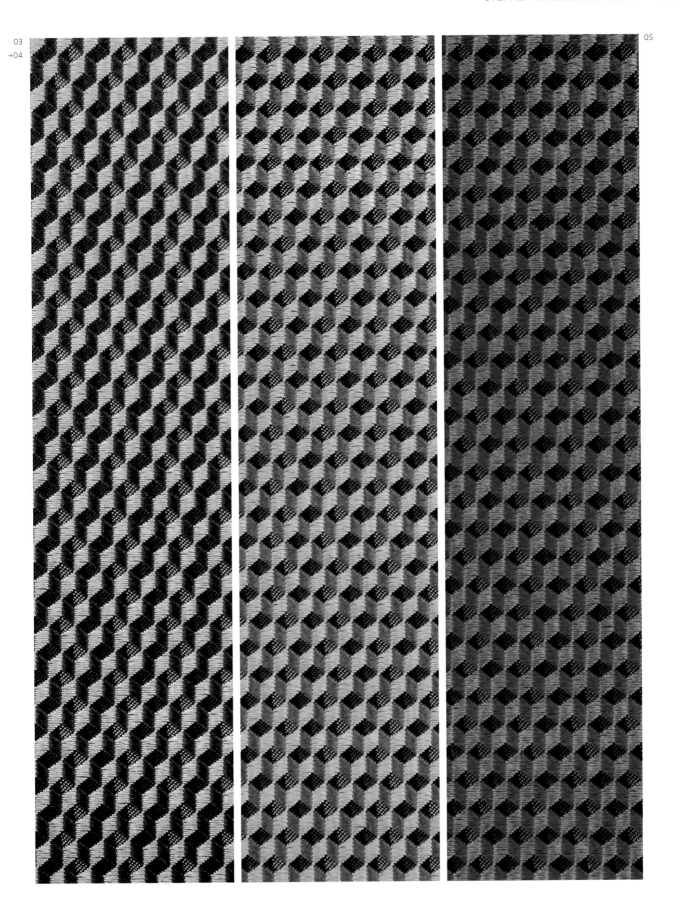

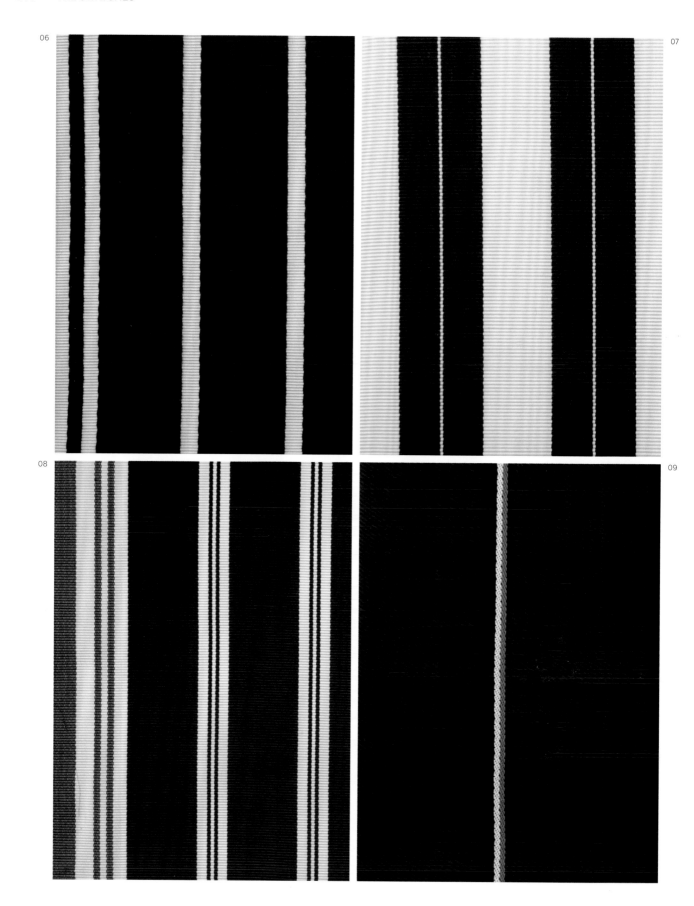

10

11

STEPHEN WALTERS AND SONS
FOR GILES

12. *Colour jacquard diffused by the introduction of mixed structures.*

13. *Variegation in jacquard colour textures to recall scales of butterfly markings.*

following pages

14. *Camouflage in jacquard silk brocade (S/S 2009).*

15. *Colour-banded jacquard leopard-skin-effect brocade (A/W 2006).*

12

14

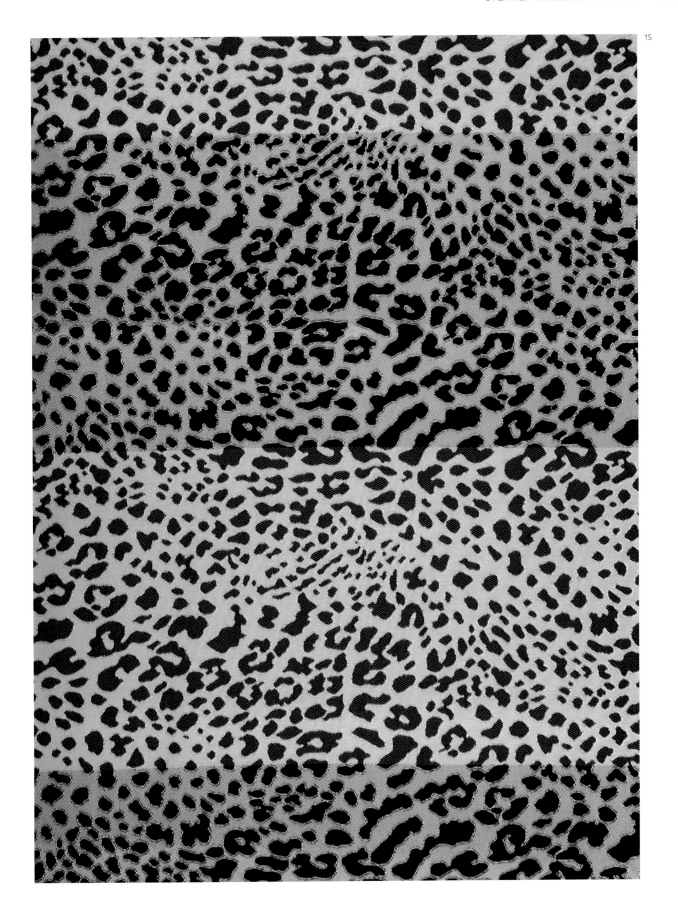

STEPHEN WALTERS AND SONS
FOR JONATHAN SAUNDERS

16. *Paisley-inspired jacquard in fuchsia and orange softened to pastel by the use of a pale warp yarn (S/S 2012).*

17. *Two-colour reversible with pale warp ground (S/S 2012).*

18. *Two-colour reversible sateen jacquard exploiting the mirroring patterns of the paisley tradition (S/S 2012).*

19. *Two-colour reversible with pale warp ground (S/S 2012).*

20. *Two-colour reversible with pale warp ground (S/S 2012).*

following pages

21. *Undulating heraldic stripe jacquard in reversible two-colour broken twill structures (S/S 2013).*

22. *Banded two-colour sateen jacquard of droplet forms in an ogee repeat (S/S 2013).*

23. *Diamond and interwoven trellis pattern in sateen jacquard (Pre-autumn 2012).*

16

17

18

19

21

22

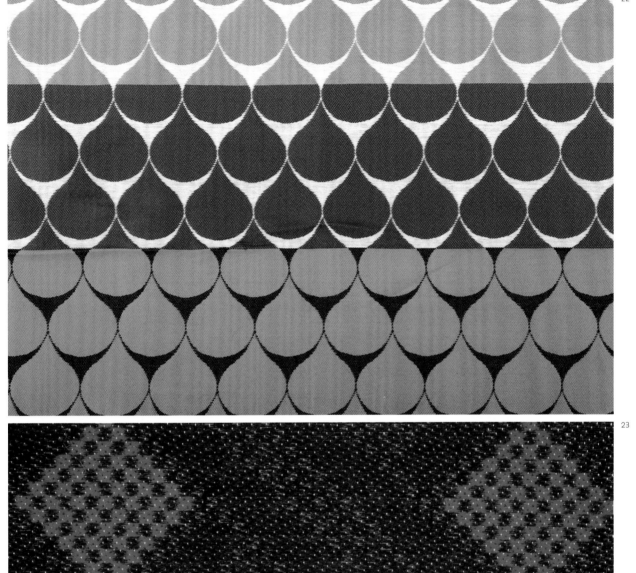

23

STEPHEN WALTERS AND SONS
FOR MARY KATRANTZOU

TECHNIQUE

The potent scale and flexibility of digital technology evidenced in printing is mirrored in contemporary electronic jacquard weaving. Freely composed figurative weaves exploit combinations of structural variegation with changes in weft yarn colour to depict large-scale patterning.

24. *Subtle effects are produced by varying the reflective quality of the fabric (A/W 2013).*

25. *Suffused photographic impressions created from a monochrome yarn palette (A/W 2013).*

26. *Computing power enables jacquard imagery to stretch the length of a garment (A/W 2013).*

27. *Architectural detail rendered as a repeating tonal pattern (RTW A/W 2013).*

28. *Jacquard impression of lace formed from the filigree structure of bridges (A/W 2013).*

24
→25

26

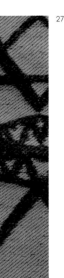

TATA NAKA

Tata Naka is designed by identical twins, Tamara and Natasha Surguladze, born in Tbilisi, Georgia, and the name of the label references their childhood nicknames. The two sisters both studied in London and they launched Tata Naka in 2002. The British Fashion Council granted the label the NEWGEN award at London Fashion Week three years in a row. With signature in-house prints based on their paintings and photography, the designers are inspired by diverse musical and artistic references, including the tribal art of West Africa, choreographer Pina Bausch, photographer Slim Aarons, 1950s romance comics and the artists Marc Chagall, Henri Matisse and Paul Gauguin. In 2010 Tata Naka celebrated its tenth anniversary with a retrospective exhibition that included a limited-edition range of T-shirts designed for London's Victoria and Albert Museum. The brand consists of two lines: Tata Naka, comprising innovative tailoring and minimal detailing, and Stolen Memories, featuring digital prints.

PHOTO-REALIST DIGITAL PRINTING
These prints from the Tata Naka Stolen Memories line use high-resolution digital photography to create hyper-real arrays of kitsch baroque patterning. The light-reflecting quality of the costume jewelry findings, charm beads and faux gems gives the *trompe l'œil* composition convincing dimensionality.

01. Trompe l'œil *digital print of beadwork and embroidery (S/S 2011).*
02. *Photoshop repetition of jewelry elements (S/S 2011).*
03. Trompe l'œil *digital print of frilled fabric (S/S 2011).*

following pages
04. *Digitally confected cornucopia of jewelled ephemera (S/S 2011).*

01

02

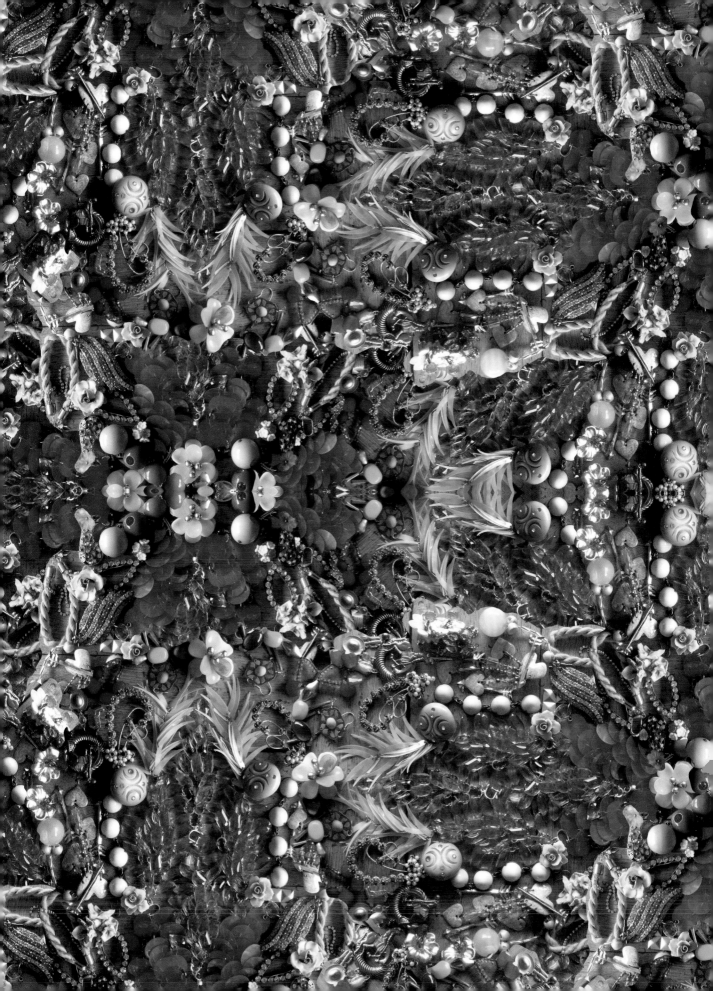

THAKOON

From its inception in 2004, the New York-based Thakoon label has created understated ready-to-wear fashion that utilizes simple silhouettes as a base for playing with pattern and texture, while also experimenting with structure and layering. Thakoon Panichgul was born in Chiang Rai Province, Thailand, and moved to Omaha, Nebraska, when he was eleven years old. With a background in business studies and fashion writing (for *Harper's Bazaar*) and after studying at Parsons The New School For Design in New York from 2001 to 2003, Thakoon attracted the attention of Anna Wintour, editor of US *Vogue*, which led to the designer winning a contract with Gap in 2007. Other collaborations include Hogan and Target in 2008, after which he launched Thakoon Addition, a second more affordable line, in 2009, followed in 2011 by Carbon Copy, a youth-oriented collection.

SCHIFFLI EMBROIDERY

The effect of flowers and butterflies appearing to float on the surface of the fabric is created by the mechanized process of schiffli, or Swiss embroidery (**01** and **02**).

01. *Schiffli-embroidered butterflies (S/S 2013).*
02. *Schiffli-embroidered floral design (S/S 2013).*
03. *Printed chiffon (A/W 2007).*
04. *Rose boutonnière print (S/S 2009).*
05. *Tumbling paper print (A/W 2009).*
06. Trompe l'œil *eyelash print (S/S 2009).*
07. *Discharge tiger print (A/W 2010).*
08. *Single-colour print (A/W 2010).*
09. *Single-colour dot print (A/W 2010).*

10. *Leavers lace over base (A/W 2011).*
11. *Red and blue plaid (A/W 2011).*
12. *Multi-directional heart print (A/W 2012).*
13. *Photo-realist digital print (A/W 2012).*
14. *Winter floral print (A/W 2013).*
15. *Pink paillettes (A/W 2013).*
16. *Digital all-over print of diffused florals (A/W 2013).*
17. *Paisley print (S/S 2012).*
18. Trompe l'œil *digital crystal print for Thakoon Addition (S/S 2006).*
19. *Polychromatic paisley print (S/S 2012).*
20. *One-directional leaf and bird print (S/S 2013).*
21. *Chinoiserie-inspired floral print (S/S 2013).*
22. *Applied raschel crochet openwork ribbon braids (S/S 2009).*

01

02

03
→04

06
05←

07
→08

10
09←

11
→12

14
13←

15
→16

18
17←

19
→20

22
21←

YAELLE

The designer behind the luxury UK-based Yaelle label was born in Britain but has roots in Tunisia and the South of France, which are both major influences to be found in her work. After the designer graduated from Manchester Metropolitan University, she gained experience in high-end fashion and developed her expertise while working for London-based labels Matthew Williamson and Roksanda Ilincic before launching the Yaelle label dedicated to creating unique hand-illustrated silk scarves. With a strong emphasis on a mixture of traditional drawing methods and contemporary printing techniques, the scarves feature highly detailed motifs culled from a variety of sources, such as the hamsa hand design, matryoshka ('babushka') dolls and decorated fans.

DIGITAL PRINTING

Digital printing is used to combine the delicacy of the hand-drawn line with complex arrangements of intense colour, all within the spatial framework prescribed by the parameters of the silk square.

01. *Hamsa hand design within a mosaic border (2012).*
02. *Koi carp over a pixelated border (2011).*
03. *Batik effect within a border of butterflies (2011).*
04. *Radial symmetry redolent of a Middle Eastern mandala (2012).*
05. *Matryoshka dolls form an inner and outer border combined with black on pink polka dots (2012).*
06. *Detailed illustration of a street scene interspersed with graphic grey stripes (2013).*

07. *Hamsa hand motif superimposed over the Union flag (2012).*

following pages
08. *Kaleidoscopic imagery includes a psychedelic version of the hamsa motif in an all-over print (2013).*

pages 368–9
09. *Fans decorated with macaroons and embroidered slippers in a sophisticated all-over design (2013).*
10. *Hand-illustrated jewelry in an all-over design (2013).*
11. *Matryoshka dolls representing cultures from around the world in an all-over design (2012).*

01
→02

03

04
→05

06

09

ZANDRA RHODES

A graduate of London's Royal College of Art at the height of the burgeoning interest in youth-led fashion, British designer Zandra Rhodes set up her first print studio in 1965 with fellow designer Alexander McIntyre. One of the most enduring and influential textile designers of the era, Rhodes initially drew inspiration from Pop art motifs and comic book images before developing her signature style, which transmuted the art and artefacts of other cultures into engineered prints. These were then incorporated into simple garment shapes, allowing the printed pattern to dictate the silhouettes of the clothing. The designer's signature 'wiggles' have remained a recurring motif since they first appeared in 1968. An early exponent of the deconstruction look, Rhodes experimented with external seams and featured construction details as decorative elements, notably producing the couture pink safety-pin dress. The designer was made a Commander of the British Empire in 1997 in recognition of her services to fashion.

COLLAGE

A composition of torn papers laid horizontally is overdrawn with rough vertical pastel lines (**02**), exemplifying a visual language that encompasses hand-worked fine art processes such as collage while being digitally printed.

01. *'Egyptian Pleating' (S/S 1987).*
02. *'Torn Stripe' (S/S 2012).*
03. *'Dandelion Digital' (S/S 2012).*

following pages
04. *'Stars'. Two-colour screen print on rayon crêpe for London-based designers Foale & Tuffin (1964).*
05. *'All-over Lipsticks'. Three-colour screen print on crêpe by Sylvia Ayton and Zandra Rhodes (1968).*

01

02

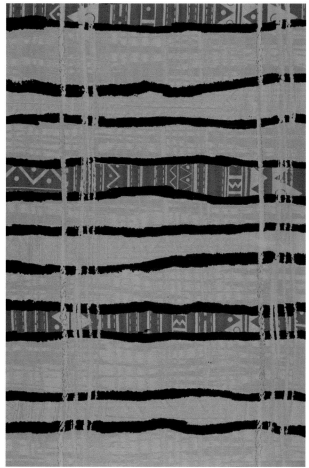

04

06

07

08

09

SCREEN-PRINTING
Rhodes reinterpreted three-dimensional chain stitch
to create the illusion of a printed knit on a flat fabric
through the medium of screen-printing (**10**).

06. *'Snail Flower And Wiggle'. Five-colour print on heavy
cotton for Vice Versa (1970).*

07. *'Knitted Flower And Wiggles'. Four-colour print for Sekers
Australia (1971).*

08. *'Wiggle And Check'. Three-colour print on satin (1970).*

09. *'Wiggle Tassel And Triangle'. Five-colour print for Sekers
Australia (1971).*

10. *'Knitted Flower And Circles'. Four-colour print for Sekers
Australia (1971).*

DIGITAL & SCREEN PRINTING
R. A. SMART

01

02

03

01. The digital printing of textiles has evolved rapidly to become a flexible and economic production technology.

02. With designs produced straight to fabric from piezo inkjet print heads, there are no screen preparation costs and no repeat limitations.

03. Designs can either originate from traditional studio media and be captured as digital images or they can be generated directly on a computer screen.

04. Different fibres demand a range of dyestuffs: acids, reactives, disperse, sublimation and pigments. These in turn require a variety of finishing processes.

05. During printing, infrared curing dries the deposited dyestuff to limit mark-off on the fabric roll.

06. Automated production allows the operator to check for misfed fabric or faults in printing.

DIGITAL & SCREEN PRINTING R. A. SMART

07. Non-repeating imagery can be scaled to conform precisely to the dimensions of the intended usage – be it a dress length, swimsuit or scarf square.

08. A pause between print runs reveals the width of the bands of minute droplets of colour that are produced by each passage of the multi-head carriage.

09. The printer is configured in line with other processing units controlled locally from the computer workstation. The computer monitors production and delivers the data as a 'rip' file.

10. The digital printer can place any mixture of designs as one image anywhere on the cloth. This facilitates economic gains in sampling or batching garment components.

11. Systems of colour fidelity monitoring are available for digital printers. Some recalibration may be necessary for different fibres or fabric structures.

12. Design data and printer settings are archived for usage on repeat orders. In the digital-printing market, order minimums are no longer burdened by screen costs.

DIGITAL & SCREEN PRINTING R. A. SMART

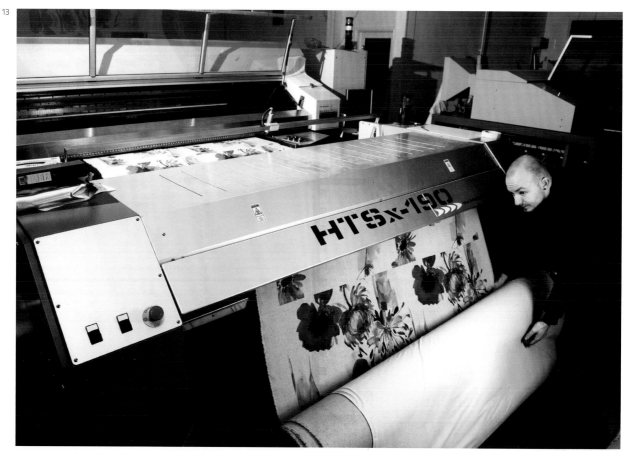

13. Printers can be aligned with drying units that evaporate the fluid base of printer inks so that the dry output can be gathered onto rolls.

14. Some dyes and fibres require other operations after printing, such as steaming. Layers of print can be isolated by paper to avoid marking.

15. The printer can add production information as text directly onto samples. This makes record keeping and cross-referencing simple.

16. Not all aspects of printing are automated; at times hand skills are preferred.

17. Some printing processes involving complex chemical applications are not available digitally, although the screens can be prepared using digital media.

18. For screen-printing efficiency and accuracy, a one-person print carriage is used for devoré, foil and discharge printing.

DISCHARGE PRINTING
FURPHY SIMPSON

See pages 146–55

01

02
→03

04

01. Original design artwork is assembled on clear film, creating opaque and transparent areas.

02. The finished montage, as a black-and-white negative, is placed on the light box.

03. The negative is checked for errors and to assess the spatial distribution of graphic elements.

04. Silk-screen stencils can be retained for further production or stripped for reuse.

05

06

07

05. An open silk screen is coated with photosensitive emulsion and left to dry.

06. An artwork negative is placed beneath a dry screen on an ultraviolet light exposure unit.

07. Ultraviolet exposure hardens emulsion in opaque areas; the remaining soft emulsion from the transparent areas is stripped out and washed away.

DISCHARGE PRINTING FURPHY SIMPSON

08. Formosul (sodium formaldehyde sulfoxylate powder) takes away the colour in dischargeable dyes.

09. Indalca, a guar gum-based thickener, is utilized to create a usable consistency for the print process.

10. Formosul and Indalca are mixed together to create the print paste for discharging colour from the dyed fabric.

11
→12

13

14

11. The appropriate length of fabric is fixed in order to accommodate the printed design.

12. The dischargeable black silk twill cloth is prepared.

13. Fabric is torn, rather than cut, from selvedge to selvedge in order to establish a straight grain.

14. The fabric is laid in accurate rectangular form on a print table treated with adhesive.

DISCHARGE PRINTING FURPHY SIMPSON

15

16
→17

18

15. The size and position of the screen are checked in relation to the fabric.

16. Prior to printing, the screen is laid down carefully in an exact position.

17. Once the screen is in position, sufficient print paste is placed outside of the design area, at the edge of the frame.

18. Different designs and fabrics require a variety of types and widths of squeegee.

19. Print paste is distributed evenly across the screen with a squeegee in preparation for printing.

20. Four passages of the squeegee ensure that the print paste goes evenly through the stencil mesh to the fabric.

21. The screen is levered away from the fabric after printing, avoiding lateral movement that would blur print.

22. Unused print paste is reclaimed for additional printing.

DISCHARGE PRINTING FURPHY SIMPSON

23. The surface residue of print paste is wiped from the silk screen mesh in the washout.

24. In order to prevent a blockage in the mesh, the screen is cleaned with cold water to remove final residue.

25. The wet printed fabric is pinned to the lath to hold the fabric open for drying.

26. The printers prepare to lift the wet printed fabric, which still has uniform colour.

27

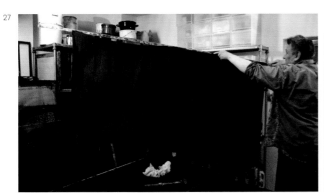

28

29

27. Printed fabric is hung to dry, before being steamed to activate the discharge effect.

28. When the fabric is dry, it is placed in a steamer and hooked onto a carousel as a spiral curtain.

29. Towels are placed on top of the carousel to prevent condensation running down onto the fabric.

DISCHARGE PRINTING FURPHY SIMPSON

30. The loaded steamer is clamped shut and left to steam for twenty minutes.

31. At the end of the process, printed fabric is removed from the steamer, revealing a visible image on the fabric.

32. The steamed fabric is unhooked from the carousel.

33

34
→35    36

33. Prior to washing, the printed fabric is laid out flat on the print table.

34. The fabric is washed by hand in hot soapy water and rinsed well to remove chemical traces.

35. The damp fabric is then ironed dry, removing creases and glazing the surface.

36. The printer reveals the finished length of fabric with the image clearly discharged out.

FULLY FASHIONED KNITWEAR
JOHN SMEDLEY

See pages 208–13

01

02

03

01. Advanced Wholegarment® technology minimizes wastage of expensive luxury yarns and provides a cost-effective and competitive method of manufacture.

02. Shima Seiki's Wholegarment® machinery was introduced in the late 1990s, providing the radical innovation of four beds of needles instead of the normal two.

03. Slender yarn carriers, programmed to traverse and descend into working position across the width of the four needle beds, are set in an arched array, focusing on the critical point of yarn delivery.

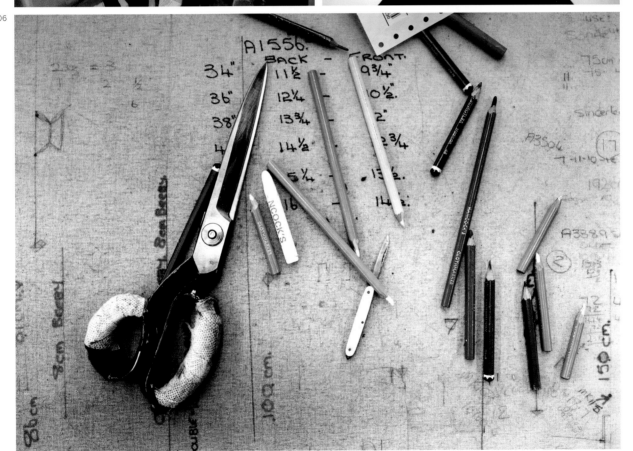

04. With fully automated electronic production, the degree of technical finesse is not diminished but rather invested in the process of perfecting prototypes, in which precise calibration can be attained and archived for instant reproduction.

05. Through the complex additive manufacturing process of Wholegarment® production, knitwear is realized in integrated three-dimensional form. These seamless garments reduce both labour costs and sensations of constriction.

06. Neck detail is incorporated directly into some seamless garments, but other styles, including fully fashioned sweaters, require the skilled hand-cutter to delineate and cut a neck opening ready for binding.

FULLY FASHIONED KNITWEAR JOHN SMEDLEY

07. As in all clothing manufacture, the relational geometry of neck aperture and shoulder line is critical to the fall and fit of knitted garments. A high degree of precision has evolved to define the hand-cutter's templates and coordinates.

08. Front-opening knitwear, such as the classic cardigan, can either be trimmed with a separate strapping or constructed with an integral button band. In both cases there remains the obligation to attach buttons with a specialized machine.

09. A misaligned button or a stretched button band will ruin an otherwise perfect garment. In order to ensure accuracy, the marking-out of the button attachment points and buttonhole locations follows a precise measure, starting from the hem.

10

11

12

10. In the manufacture of luxury knitwear, batch size is relatively limited. Consequently, all skilled sewing hands on the production line may encounter a variety of garment colours in a day's work

11. Among the most valued skills in making high-quality knitted goods is linking or binding. This type of sewing process allows panels and trims to be attached with great precision.

12. The radial linking machine has points that anchor the work while a chain stitch binds components with a chain link at each point. On collars, the cut neck is sandwiched within a folded rib, with each open loop placed on a point.

FULLY FASHIONED KNITWEAR JOHN SMEDLEY

13. Some fully fashioned knitwear, such as Sea Island cotton T-shirts, has a tubular welt or turned hem on each panel. This allows the hem to remain flat but it requires hand-sewing, or grafting, to close the side seams.

14. The skill of hand-finishing staff compares with that of the couture ateliers in Paris. Long-standing quality manufacturers in the UK have often insisted on training staff for six months before allowing them to touch production.

15. Fine-gauge shaped knitwear in delicate natural fibres, such as merino lambswool and Sea Island cotton, can be susceptible to defects from natural variegation in raw material or stress in production. Quality monitoring is imperative.

16. A multicoloured striped jacquard sweater, produced by the fully fashioned method, is prepared for final pressing on an angled steam bed. As a first step, an articulated former is inserted through the neck opening.

17. Once held in correct shape and to size by the metal former, the garment is subjected to steam from below and smoothed with a padded blade as a vacuum draws away the water vapour. Steam relaxes the fibres.

18. When the garment is finished, and all quality assurance checks have been completed, specific data relating to each piece is recorded for cataloguing and archival purposes.

HAND EMBROIDERY
HAND & LOCK

See pages 162–7

01

02
→03

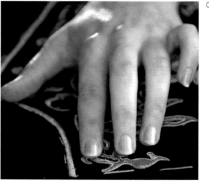

04

1. The threads that are used industrially for bespoke hand embroidery are also sought by amateur enthusiasts for their highest quality handiwork. The fidelity to shade and the reliability of colour fastness are paramount.

2. Even in goldwork, it is necessary to combine machine and hand stitching to attain the required effect in certain designs.

3. On a ground of velvet, Irish machine embroidery is given a raised outline detail by hand. Irish embroidery is used to build up pattern with chain stitch in a similar manner to crewelwork.

4. Pearl purl thread – also known as Jaceron – is a hollow metal spiral that is couched to the ground fabric by drawing a sewing thread in between the coils of the metal yarn.

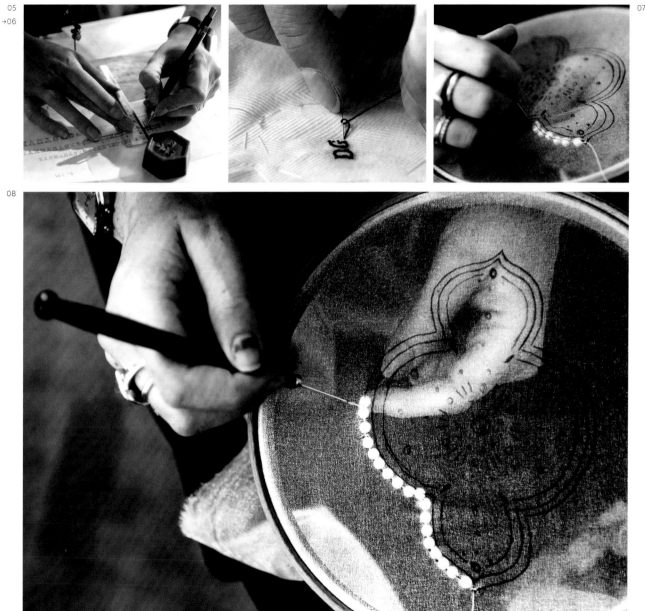

5. The simplicity of a monogram demands the highest precision in drafting as any inaccuracy is amplified by the expanse of clear fabric in the background.

6. The monogram is realized with silk thread in a variation on stem stitch, which particularly lends itself to the controlled curves and exact angles required for lettering. Additional loops of thread can be added to stem stitch to build texture.

7. Tambour beading is a technique that employs a hooked needle, known as a tambour hook, to catch the threaded beads underneath the fabric stretched in a frame. The name 'tambour' is derived from the drum-like embroidery frame.

8. The design motif is delineated on the sheer chiffon fabric as a guide to the attachment of the threaded beads, which are caught by a chain stitch worked from the back.

HAND EMBROIDERY HAND & LOCK

9. For the process of constructing plaited epaulettes and shoulder boards, nails are configured in a precise pattern as a jig for the intertwining of rotund braided cords that are composed of 2 per cent gold.

10. The interlacing of the gold cords involves looping both within and between layers in order to achieve the complex knots. At the end of the process, immaculate splicing is required to hide the cut ends of the cord.

11. Since the 18th century, epaulettes in both gold and silver cord have been used to denote rank in military and ceremonial apparel. Subtle hierarchical nuances were invested in whether the left or right shoulder, or both, was adorned.

12. Drafting the graphic layout for a symbolic piece, such as the coat of arms of Prince William, Duke of Cambridge, demands a close understanding of and rigid adherence to the protocols of the iconography.

13. A needle is used to create holes along the lines of the draft in order to enable the design to be pounced onto the fabric. Creating these perforations is known as pricking the design or making the pricking pattern.

14. The design is transferred to the cloth as spots of powder, ready for embroidery. The pounce (usually crushed cuttlefish for darker fabrics and charcoal for lighter fabrics) is pushed through the perforations using felt in a circular motion.

15. When the pricking pattern is peeled away after pouncing, the detailed layout of the design is revealed on the fabric beneath, ready for the needlework processes to begin.

HAND EMBROIDERY HAND & LOCK

16. When using strong thread to secure a panel of fabric in a goldwork stretcher frame, damage to the delicate yarns of the base cloth caused by friction is reduced by lubricating the sewing thread with beeswax.

17. Stretcher frames are used for goldwork because they have a metal support to keep the embroidery tight and stable. The fabric is attached to the frame with a cross-hatched basting stitch in a strong thread.

18. When the fabric for goldwork has been mounted to the frame, it is put under careful tension by means of the stretcher screw to create a pucker-free base for the needlework.

19. The gilt rough bullion is employed for goldwork essing – a technique that gives the illusion that the bullion yarn is entwined together – which resembles a multitude of little 'S' shapes.

20. An assortment of skeins of coloured silk thread are ready to be used in hand embroidery.

21. Densely packed areas of chain stitch are realized with the Cornelly machine, which uses a hooked needle and a circular machine foot. This allows controlled free travel of the fabric in relation to the hooked needle as it makes its chains.

22. The Cornelly machine has to be guided entirely by hand to produce patterning in chain stitch. Its operation demands the highest level of skilled hand–eye coordination.

HAND-WEAVING
DASHING TWEEDS

See pages 116–19

01

02
→03

04

01. The core impact of tweed hinges on the rich interplay of blended yarn colours with woven microstructures.

02. The preparation of the longitudinal threads for the sample is effected by winding the warp yarn in lateral sequence around a pegged warping mill.

03. At the end of each lap of the rotating warping mill, threads are passed in a figure of eight path around separation pegs to protect the true sequence.

04. The warp threads are transferred from the warping mill to the beam of the loom where they are tensioned consistently.

05. On a dobby loom – be it mechanical or electronic – the structure sequences are produced by selectively lifting shafts with heddles that are loaded with individual warp threads.

06. Heddles are ranged across the shaft in a sequence that relates to the heddles on other shafts, following the threading plan and working with the lifting plan of the pattern.

07. Working across the width of the warp, threads passing from the warp beam are drawn through the heddles by hand.

HAND-WEAVING DASHING TWEEDS

08. A small threading hook is inserted into the eye of the heddle in order to pull through individual warp threads in sequence.

09. When all the heddles for the threading plan have been drawn in, they should remain parallel and without crossovers.

10. After the heddles have been loaded, the parallel warp threads are spaced out across the loom in the gaps (dents) of the reed, held in the batten.

11

12
→13

14

11. The process of threading the reed is known as 'sleying' and the weaver uses a fine reed hook. The spacing of reeds is variable and the choice of reed dictates the sett, or thread density, of the warp.

12. Warp threads are prevented from slipping back through the reed by simply knotting off small groups with a slip knot.

13. The final step of warp preparation is to attach the threads beyond the reed batten to the apron rod of the cloth beam, which is tensioned with a ratchet let-off device.

14. The transverse weft yarns are wound onto small pirns, or bobbins, for insertion into the shuttle.

HAND-WEAVING DASHING TWEEDS

15. Quality shuttles are made from fine-grained boxwood in order to reduce friction in the passage across the loom. As the shuttle crosses the warp, the pirn rotates, releasing yarn for the weft.

16. The electronic selection system is harnessed to a foot-treadle mechanism, which lifts the desired shaft for each weft pick of the pattern, thus allowing the shuttle to pass under selected warp threads.

17. The weaver sits at the loom making the fabric pick by pick by passing the weft across the warp with the shuttle and beating up the weft with the reed in the batten device.

18. The selected shafts are lifted by the treadle mechanism, creating a 'shed' for the weft to pass through in the shuttle.

19. The weft yarn is drawn in an arc across the width of the warp shed in order to provide a margin of ease when the threads interweave in low relief.

20. The face side of the cloth is defined according to the travel of the twill from bottom left to top right. This arises from the habit of drafting the threading plan from the left-hand corner.

21. It is preferable to maintain a smooth selvedge on the sample, as any distortion can produce buckling of the surface across the entire width as a result of differential tension.

22. Samples can be retrieved before the entire length of warp has been consumed by cutting away at the cloth-beam end and then reconnecting the warp to the apron.

JACQUARD WEAVING
STEPHEN WALTERS AND SONS

See pages 344–57

01

02
→03

04

01. Horizontal (weft) coloured threads in patterned jacquard fabrics are delivered into the loom directly from coned packages of yarn.

02. A weft accumulator is used to create an even-tensioned reservoir of yarn from which the rapier, or projectile, can draw weft to insert across the warp.

03. Many jacquard fabrics require the warp yarns to reappear as weft, inserted transversely. Yarn for weft – and for replacing broken warp ends – is kept on racks near to the loom.

04. Within the complex synchronized motions of the jacquard loom, the most dynamic is the insertion of delicate weft yarn at high cycle speeds across the warp. This operation requires expert supervision.

05
→06

07

08

05. The jacquard harness is mounted in a gantry above the loom. From this, thousands of inextensible cords, distributed evenly by the cumber board, descend to provide for the raising of individual warp yarns to create pattern.

06. Warp yarn is delivered to the point of interweaving – the raised shed – from wound beams, through the heddles of the jacquard harness and through the reed of the beater. The lateral weft threads pass through the fingers of the weft selector unit.

07. In order to maintain fidelity to the intended design, every warp yarn has to be threaded precisely to the correct heddle, connected up to the jacquard harness.

08. The weaver supervises looms placed face to face within the avenue that is created by the heavy superstructure of the jacquard gantry. At the beginning of production, the loom-tackler makes subtle adjustments for quality.

JACQUARD WEAVING STEPHEN WALTERS AND SONS

09. In jacquard fabrics, pattern is expressed by a complexity of yarn colour and variations in fine structures. Every line, or pick, of pattern requires an instantaneous lift of selected yarns in the warp.

10. As silk fabrics are woven densely – with many qualities having a hundred threads (ends) per centimetre – the cords from the jacquard harness form a serried forest of layers.

11. Pattern variegation can be enhanced in a jacquard fabric by using a striped warp. This produces a reduction of flexibility between production runs and would necessitate larger orders or higher costs.

12. In order to be able to stop the loom in the case of a broken end, every thread in the warp passes under a light metal dropper that can fall to make electrical contact with a metal bar stop-motion device.

13. To facilitate splicing in a supplementary matching thread to support a broken end, small cones of warp colours are tied across the rear side, or beam end, of the loom.

14. A broken end in the warp is restored by knotting in a length of identical thread and passing it through all the elements of the yarn path of the warp, at the same tension as all the other ends.

15. To re-enter a broken thread, the weaver or tackler uses a long slender hook to pass the yarn through the range of apertures that constitute the yarn path.

JACQUARD WEAVING STEPHEN WALTERS AND SONS

16. The reconnection of a broken end of the finest silk to the warp requires perfect knotting under perfect tension, using a weaver's knot.

17. The strength, gloss and lightweight fineness of silk make possible highly detailed graphic patterning, rendered in combinations of woven structures.

18. A narrow band of stronger yarns is inserted at the edges from small beams to make a 'mock leno' selvedge, holding the weft yarn at the full width before being cut free.

19. A fault is traced in the warp yarn from the beam end of the loom, which is aligned back to back with the next rank of looms.

20. In order to retain the end-on-end sequence of the threading of the warp, the yarn is kept in a figure-of-eight crossover as it passes forwards to the shed point.

21. The maintenance of consistent tension through the exact yarn path demands keen expertise.

22. The weaver's knot creates a quick and effective linkage when applied with dexterity.

JACQUARD WEAVING STEPHEN WALTERS AND SONS

23

24
→25

26

23. As yarns cross from the weft accumulator to the weft selection fingers, they pass through ceramic eyelets in a device that senses breaks in yarn motion by induction.

24. A striped tie silk is carried from the loom for further processing, still wrapped around the take-off roller.

25. A weft thread is reinstated through the induction motion sensor onto the selection drop fingers.

26. The creel of the weft accumulator is loaded with a fresh package of the correct yarn and colour.

27. The yarn is drawn through the accumulator with a flexible plastic hook before the unit winds a reserve of thread under a calibrated tension.

28. Each weft selection drop finger is fed yarn from an individual weft accumulator.

29. Despite a high degree of automation and the transition to digital control, the use of silk, a natural fibre with natural irregularities, demands close supervision during production.

30. The simpler the design, the greater the vigilance needed to monitor for small defects that could render the final piece substandard.

LACE
CLUNY LACE

See pages 90–7

01. A reel is loaded with empty bobbins for threading. Each bobbin comprises two joined circular plates of thin brass.

02. Yarn is threaded and wound inside the narrow bobbins. A skilled hand is able to wind up to one hundred bobbins at a time.

03. Bobbin yarn is very fine and the threading process is as demanding as it would be to thread one hundred sewing needles simultaneously.

04. The reel, loaded with threaded bobbins, is mounted on the winding machine in order to fill each bobbin with up to 80 metres (262 ft) of yarn.

05. Yarns run under careful tension from a creel, or rack, of bulky packages to the slender lace bobbins on the reel.

06. The reel of bobbins is monitored constantly during winding in order to eliminate mishaps.

07. Filled yarn bobbins have to be pressed and put into an oven to make sure that they are perfectly flat. This ensures safe passage between the beam threads on the machine.

LACE CLUNY LACE

08. The finest Egyptian cotton is fed from a creel of individual cones onto a beam on the beaming mill.

09. Yarn tensioning devices on the beaming mill.

10. Yarn beams at the back of the machine – each end is threaded through the machine.

11. Threads delivered from beams in the Leavers machine are of different gauges, depending on whether they are used for 'outline' or 'filling in'.

12. In order to produce the lace structure, bobbins are transported between the beam yarns in narrow carriages.

13. Individual bobbins must be threaded manually into the bobbin carriages.

14. Empty carriages wait to be threaded with circular bobbins filled with yarn.

LACE CLUNY LACE

15. Loaded bobbins are threaded into carriages.

16. The craft of twisthand requires complex skills - such as the ability to reunite broken threads within the lace pattern – and training extends over seven years.

17. When a thread breaks free, it is lifted back through the delicate mechanisms of the machine to reconnect with the design.

18. Punched pasteboard cards – or jacquard cards – control the patterning movements of the lace machine and the yarns to create the design.

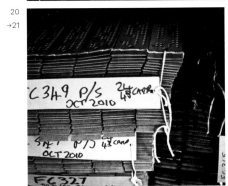

19. Jacquard card sets are unique to individual designs and they are cross-referenced carefully to fabric archives.

20. Jacquard card sets are also prepared to produce new designs.

21. Two twisthands work together to change the set-out on a machine. This involves threading up the machine with more than ten thousand threads.

22. Excess yarn is cut away as threads are brought up through the machine.

LACE CLUNY LACE

23

24
→25

26

23. Before the machine is put under power, it is advanced manually in order to check that the interlinking and alignment of threads are correct.

24. Part of the preparation of the subtle mechanisms of the lace machine is checking that all the bobbins are under the same tension.

25. The machine is advanced slowly to allow the twisthand to inspect the face side of the lace-work.

26. Broken threads have to be tied up into the fabric otherwise they will lead to unwanted holes in the lace.

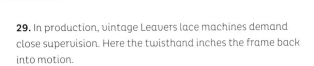

27. The face of work: bands of lace are made together on the machine and separated later, after dyeing and finishing, to make an individual lace trim.

28. Leavers lace machines were originally powered by steam-driven belt networks, which dictated the alleyway layout of the mills.

29. In production, vintage Leavers lace machines demand close supervision. Here the twisthand inches the frame back into motion.

LACE CLUNY LACE

30. The yarn beam rack delivers individual threads, spaced out laterally, thus allowing the bobbin carriages to operate between the base net yarns.

31. The jacquard punched-card mechanism activates the motion-selection system of the lace machine, permitting patterned designs.

32. Maintaining the smooth flow of the pasteboard pattern-card chain through the jacquard harness is critical to accurate design realization.

33. Elements of the delicate jacquard selection apparatus are adjusted.

34. Lace is dyed and finished in wide panels before separation and profiling by hand.

35. Lace is cut by hand following the scalloped design profile.

36. The placement of lace trim onto a card ready for dispatch is known as 'jennying'.

GLOSSARY

2/2 TWILL

A type of weave with a pattern of diagonal parallel ribs, 2/2 twill is achieved by passing the weft thread over one or more warp threads and then under two or more warp threads and so on, with a 'step', or offset, between rows to create the characteristic diagonal pattern.

ADHESION OF REFLECTIVE PLASTIC LAMINATES AND CRYSTAL CABOCHONS

Traditionally cabochons are polished gemstones but they can also be created from hand-moulded crystal using classic glass-making techniques. These flat-backed items and nacreous shell laminates may be glued or fused onto most textile materials using a variety of heat-setting and ultrasonic welding techniques.

APPLIQUÉ

Textile appliqué is a technique in which pieces of fabric are sewn or glued onto another piece of fabric to create designs, patterns and pictures.

BOHUS HAND-KNITTING

Founded in 1939 by a group of women from the north of Bohuslän, Sweden, Bohus Stickning provided a home-based industry for a community that was economically depressed by the closure of local quarries. The garments feature intricate plain and purl patterning of stranded colour, similar in effect to Fair Isle and intarsia. The company evolved from a small enterprise to produce international high-end quality designs. Production ceased in the region in 1969.

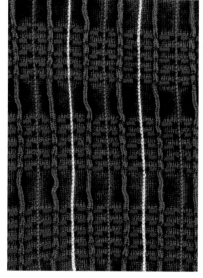

BOUCLÉ

A type of yarn featuring a length of loops of similar size ranging from small to large circles. To make bouclé, at least two strands of yarn are combined with differing tensions. Bouclé can also refer to the fabric that is made from this type of yarn; it maintains the looped appearance.

BRIOCHE KNITTING

Brioche knitting involves tucked stitches, i.e. yarn overs that are knitted

together with a slipped stitch from the previous row. Such stitches may also be made by knitting into the row below (equivalent to the slipped stitch) and dropping the stitch above (equivalent to the yarn over).

BROCADE

Brocade may be mistaken for embroidery because of its decorative surface but it is woven on a loom. An extra weft produces the figuring and illuminates the floral pattern. The word 'brocade' is now used loosely to describe any jacquard-woven design.

BUGLE BEADS

Bugle beads are a variety of a 'seed bead', a generic term for any small bead. Bugle beads are longer than they are wide, creating a tubular shape.

BULLION THREAD

Used in goldwork embroidery, bullion threads are very fine tubular-shaped wire threads. The bullion threads consist of a hollow, soft and flexible metal tube, and this is cut into pieces and sewn down like a bead.

CABLE STITCH

A knitting technique, cable stitch requires two or more groups of adjacent vertical columns of loops to pass under and over one another giving the effect of a plaited rope.

CASHMERE

A luxurious 'noble' fibre, cashmere was originally hair from the downy undercoat of the Asiatic goat (*Capra hircus laniger*) with a mean diameter of 18.5 micrometres or less. Similar hair from animals bred selectively from the feral goat populations of Australia, New Zealand and Scotland is regarded as cashmere provided that the fibre diameter is similar. The finest cashmere, however, is from China and it originates from a small district to the west of Beijing and another in Manchuria. It gives warmth without weight and, although it does not have the elastic, resilient quality of wool from a sheep, it has perfect draping qualities.

CHAIN STITCH

A surface embellishment, chain stitch is an embroidery technique in which a series of looped stitches form a chain-like pattern. Chain stitches are also used in making tambour lace, needle lace, macramé and crochet.

CHAINETTE YARN

This yarn is constructed from a series of interlocking chains that provide both lightness and strength.

CHAPA SILK

A medium- to lightweight raw slubby silk.

CHIFFON

A fine lightweight transparent fabric with a smoothness and drape that may be woven in silk, cotton or a synthetic fibre.

CHINÉ YARN

Chiné is used to describe yarns, and occasionally fabrics, that have two colours closely intertwined. Examples include 'mottled' and 'marled', but not 'mouliné' or 'mélange'. These latter terms imply a more intimate mingling of colours, with possibly more than two colour components.

CHENILLE

Chenille yarn is manufactured by placing short lengths of yarn, called the 'pile', between two core yarns and then twisting the yarns together. The edges of these piles then stand at right angles to the yarn's core, giving chenille its typically tufted appearance.

CLOQUE

A cotton, silk or rayon fabric with a raised woven pattern and a blistered or quilted look.

CORDONNET GIMP

A narrow ornamental braid made of silk, wool or cotton, cordonnet gimp is often stiffened with metallic wire or has a coarse cord running through it.

COUCHING

This simple hand-embroidery technique involves two threads: a laid thread, the thread that is being couched onto the fabric, and a working thread, the thread that holds the laid thread onto the fabric. A plain couching stitch involves a small straight stitch taken over the laid thread.

CRAQUELURE

In textiles, the technique of craquelure is commonly used to create an artificially aged or distressed surface. This requires an inflexible laminated or glossy pigment to be applied to the base cloth, which then dries and cracks under heat or as the result of a chemical reaction.

CRÊPE DE CHINE

A lightweight fabric, crêpe de Chine has an all-silk warp and weft or a silk warp with a hard-spun worsted weft. The crêpe effect is created by the use of weft, or filling, yarns spun with the twist running in reverse directions and known as right-hand and left-hand twist, respectively. During the finishing operation, because of the abnormal amount of twist in the picks of filling, the yarns tend to untwist and recover their normal condition, thereby causing the characteristic surface of typical crêpe de Chine.

CREPONNE CLOTH

Creponne cloth is characterized by lengthwise wrinkles and it is woven on dobby or jacquard looms. It features a sturdy, vertically rippled texture and may be silk, synthetic fibre, wool or cotton.

CUTWORK

Also known as whitework, cutwork involves removing threads from a woven background and then wrapping or filling the remaining holes with embroidery.

DEVORÉ

Devoré, or burnout, describes a process of chemically destroying (and thus removing) a component of a composite fabric of cellulose fibres, such as cotton, linen or rayon. Cellulose is decomposed by acid; the most commonly used chemical is sodium bisulphate, which develops mild sulphuric acid when heated. The devoré can be resisted with bicarbonate of soda or soda ash (both mild alkalis) in a thickened solution.

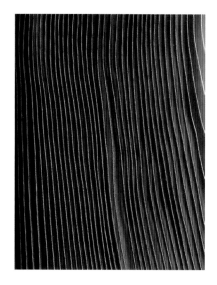

DISCHARGE PRINTING

Also known as extract printing, the technique is a method of applying a design to dyed fabric by printing a colour-destroying agent, such as chlorine or hydrosulphite, to bleach out a white or light pattern on a darker coloured ground. The dischargeable ground colour can also be replaced with an illuminating colour in the same process.

DOBBY WEAVING

In dobby weaving, the maximum number of warp-thread selections is determined by the number of shafts of heddles that the loom possesses: from just two to thirty-two. The cloth is characterized by small geometric patterns and extra texture.

DOGSTOOTH/HOUNDSTOOTH CHECK

A tessellated two-colour textile pattern characterized by broken checks or abstract four-pointed shapes, houndstooth, houndstooth check or hound's tooth is also known as dogstooth, dogtooth or dog's tooth.

EMBOSSED LEATHER

Tooling, stamping and embossing are terms that refer to the craft of impressing three-dimensional images onto leather to give a raised appearance. The tooling and embossing process is only suitable for vegetable-tanned leather, which is also often called tooling leather. Once the design has been created, it is transferred with a stylus from a tracing film onto dampened leather. The outline is then traced over with a swivel knife, which has to be kept upright at a 90-degree angle to the skin, deep enough to penetrate the grain. The leather is placed on a marble slab and pressure from a wooden or rawhide mallet is applied to various tools in order to add texture to the piece and to create depressions in the surface. Some low-relief patterning can be achieved by the use of cut-metal dies that are applied to the hide in a press.

ENGINEERED DIGITALLY PRINTED TEXTILES

Engineered or placement prints are designed to fit the pattern piece, rather than the design being printed onto a continuous length of cloth.

This approach has become widespread in contemporary fashion design due to the inherent flexibility and immediacy of digital printing.

FAIR ISLE

The typical patterning of the original Fair Isle is made up of horizontal bands of colour, usually fewer than fifteen rows deep. The separation of circular motifs by four diagonal corners produces the so-called 'OXO' design, the 'X' with a vertical line running through its centre. The simplest method of knitting a coloured pattern is to work together two threads of different colours, stranding the unused yarn behind the working yarn at each stitch. No more than two or three colours can be used, as the strands would be too long for practicality. The resulting double thickness of a jumper knitted in this style provides ideal protection against the damp and cold climate of Northern Europe because it is warm and flexible yet durable.

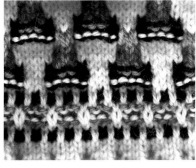

FIL COUPÉ

Fil coupé is created by extra floating wefts embodied in a fabric, particularly a jacquard, that can be cut to produce a fringe effect.

FLÉCHAGE

Fléchage is a term used in knitting and it means bending or flexing the normally straight vertical rows (wales) of stitches. This can happen in two ways: i) by repeatedly transferring (laterally) groups of stitches to make lace. This also occurs at the selvedge in full-fashioning; ii) by distorting the fabric through making incomplete rows of knitting in specific zones (also known as 'holding' or 'short course knitting').

FOULARD

A silk or a mix of silk and cotton, a lightweight twill or a plain woven fabric, foulard is usually printed with a small-scale pattern in a basic block repeat. In modern French, '*foulard*' is also the word for a scarf or neckerchief.

FULLY FASHIONED KNITTING

In 1864, William Cotton of Leicestershire, England, developed a machine to make fully fashioned knitwear that produced shaped garment pieces. When knitting, altering the number of stitches in a row widens or narrows the garment panel. An increase is achieved by moving outer loops sideways on a frame and creating extra loops. This process leaves a small eyelet hole in the fabric known as a fashioning mark. When decreasing, the process is reversed and the loops move inwards. This time the fashioning mark appears where two loops are compressed into one new loop. The final pattern pieces are sewn together using the processes of linking or cup seaming to form a chain-stitched seam along the closed selvedges inside the garment. Garments shaped in this way are known as fully fashioned and are regarded as high quality. Occasionally some firms use fake fashioning marks to make garments appear to be fully fashioned rather than cut and sewn.

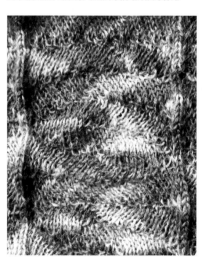

GALLOON

A galloon is a decorative woven trim, sometimes in the form of a braid, and it is commonly made of metallic gold or silver thread, lace or embroidery. Galloon is frequently used as a trim in military and police uniforms and ecclesiastical dress.

GEORGETTE

A very sheer, lightweight fabric woven from silk, cotton or synthetic yarns.

GOLDWORK

Originally developed in Asia and in use for more than two thousand years, goldwork is the art of surface embroidery using metal threads. An expensive and time-consuming task, it is usually reserved for ceremonial garb, the military and high-end fashion items. It is known as goldwork because the metal wires used to make the threads are gold-coated (silver gilt); cheaper metals such as silver and even copper are also used. The vast majority of goldwork is a form of laid work or couching, in which the gold threads are held on to the surface of the fabric by a second thread, usually of silk. The ends of the thread, depending on type, are cut off or pulled through to the back of the embroidery and carefully secured with the couching thread. A mellore or a stiletto tool is used to help position the threads and to create the holes needed to pull them through.

GOSSAMER

An extremely light and delicate variety of gauze.

GUIPURE LACE

A heavy lace in which the elements of the pattern are connected by fine threads, or brides, rather than being supported on a net ground. Often layered with overlapping motifs, guipure lace is constructed on a water-soluble or heat-resistant base that is then removed.

HAND-KNITTING

Hand-knitted garments are divided into two types: 'flat', which has a selvedge, and 'circular', in which the side edges have been joined. In flat knitting, the knitter generally knits with two needles from right to left on one side of the fabric, turns the work (over) and then knits right to left back to the start. In circular pieces, the yarns are passed in a spiral manner along multiple needles that have no end stop. There are a variety of possible stitches. A piece of knitting begins with the process of casting-on, which involves the creation of the stitches on the needle. Once the piece is finished, the remaining live stitches are cast off to close the panel.

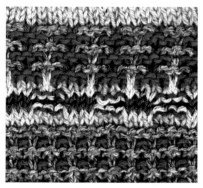

IKAT WEAVING

Ikat (from the Malay word *mengikat*, meaning 'to tie') is a type of weaving in which the warp or weft, or both, is tie-dyed before being woven to create a distinctive feathered edge to the imagery. The precision of the wrapped yarn determines the clarity of the design. After wrapping, the warp threads are dyed. When finished and unwrapped, the areas under the ties remain the original colour. Numerous colours can be added after additional wrappings.

INTARSIA KNITTING

The intarsia technique equates to knitted tapestry and is a method of free patterning that deploys two or more colours within the same course on weft-knitted plain, rib or purl fabrics. The word 'intarsia' originates from the creation of patterns in furniture using wood inlay called intersio. This craft technique was brought to Italy from the Middle East in the 15th century by the Certosini monks.

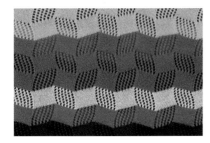

JACQUARD WEAVING

Complex patterns are created by varying the sequence in which the warp threads are raised and lowered. The jacquard loom was developed by Joseph-Marie Jacquard in 1804 and permitted the control of each warp thread individually.

LAMÉ

A fabric woven with metallic threads that catch the light to give an impression of silver, gold or copper.

LASER-CUTTING

Laser-cutting hinges upon the delivery of a highly focused, intensified blade of light to the material to be cut or engraved. The optical trajectory of the laser beam follows precise vector paths, controlled by digital step motors that can be accurate to one micron. Inert compressed nitrogen is often used to minimize char with organic materials such as leather and suede.

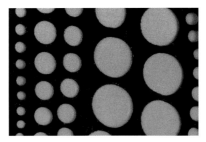

LATTICEWORK

A composite filling stitch used on plain and even weave base fabrics, often worked in two contrasting colours.

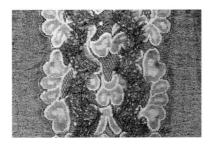

LINO-CUTTING

A printmaking technique in which the surface of linoleum (a composite sheet material with a burlap backing) is excised with various tools to produce either a positive or negative print. The tools can be used to cut the main shape in outline or to cut away the surrounding areas, leaving the outline in relief. The raised areas of the block are then inked with a roller and the paper is laid on top or printed on a flat base. In each case, pressure is applied.

LUREX

Lurex is the registered brand name of a reflective yarn that is made from synthetic film onto which a metallic aluminium, silver or gold layer has been vaporized. Lurex may also refer to cloth that is created using the yarn.

MACHINE-KNITTED FABRIC

Hand-knitting became mechanized in 1589 with the invention of the stocking knitting frame by William Lee of Nottinghamshire. It was a process that was confined initially to hosiery, which at the time also included underwear. Machine-knitted garments are either fully fashioned or cut and sewn from a length of knitted fabric. Knitted fabric gains its flexibility from the loop structure that stretches and moulds to fit body shapes. The interlocking of a series of loops, or stitches, is created either by hand or machine. The loops are interlocked using a needle to hold the existing loop while a new loop is formed in front of the old loop. The old loop is then brought over the new loop to form the fabric. Knitting differs from weaving in that a single piece of yarn can be used to create the entire length of fabric or the entire garment. The fabric consists of horizontal rows known as courses and vertical columns of loops known as wales.

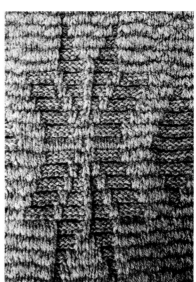

MACHINE-MADE LEAVERS LACE

Invented in the city of Nottingham, England, at the beginning of the 19th century, Leavers lace machines were smuggled to France where, with the later addition of a jacquard system, they were used to produce lace that was previously made by hand. A Leavers machine is in fact two machines: one is based on the principle invented by John Leavers in 1813, which twists together the threads to form a ground net, and the other is a jacquard machine, developed between 1836 and 1841, which applies the pattern.

MACRAMÉ

Macramé is a form of textile making achieved by tying cordage into knots. Among a variety of simple and complex knots, the most basic are the square knot and various forms of 'hitching': full hitch and double half hitches.

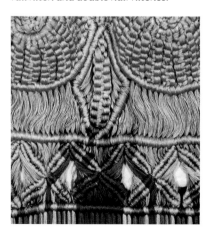

MERINO WOOL

Merino sheep were originally a Spanish breed and they produce wool that is noted for its whiteness and softness. Lambswool is from the first year's clip and merino from the second. Merino wool is considered the most valuable of wools and Australia now produces about 43 per cent of the world's supply.

META-TRANS PRINTING

The imagery is screen-printed in adhesive onto the fabric. A metallic foil is then attached by heat to the imagery and the residual foil removed.

MOIRÉ

A ribbed woven silk that is finished by being run through rollers. This process crushes the rib in different directions and gives the fabric a visible watermark effect.

NEEDLEPOINT LACE

A lace made using a needle and thread. This is the most flexible of the lace-making techniques and it is considered by some to be the highest form of the art. *Punto in aria* (stitch in the air), or needlepoint lace, developed in the 15th century. Stitches were basted onto pattern over parchment paper. A simple buttonhole stitch was used to cover and connect the pattern threads, thus creating the lace. The connecting stitches between the motifs are called 'brides' because they 'marry' the motifs.

OMBRÉ

Ombré is a dip-dye effect and the term is often used to describe fabric in which the shades of colour graduate from light to dark or segue from one contrasting colour to another.

ORGANZA

A transparent fabric that is both heavy and stiff. Organza holds its form well, making dramatic shapes, and is woven from rayon.

PAILLETTE

An oversized metal or plastic sequin.

PAINTING ON SILK

The ground fabric is stretched taut onto to a frame, and the design is then either free painted or the outline is drawn with guttering or a tjanting tool, a pen-like tool used for applying melted wax to the fabric to control the spread of the dyes. Once the outline has dried, the dyes are added to build up layers of colour. Once the dyes are dry, heat is used to fix the fabric.

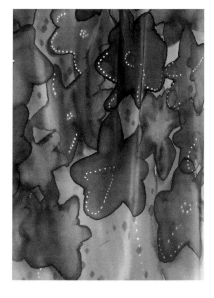

PINTUCKING

A pintuck is a pleat or fold of fabric that has been stitched into place. Pintucks are usually created in a group, with each tuck parallel to the next. Typically each fold in a group is the same size, although a change in size or direction can be used to create special visual effects.

PLACEMENT PRINTS

Placement prints usually concern a single motif. The prints can be printed before or after the garment is sewn together, depending on how the print interacts with the seam lines.

PLISSÉ

An intentionally puckered finish given to fabric by treating it with a caustic soda, such as sodium hydroxide solution, or through tension weaving. Both processes tighten the fabric in the areas where the puckering or creasing is desired. From the French *plisser*, meaning 'to pleat', the word can be used either to denote the finish of the fabric or the fabric itself.

RASCHEL KNIT

A lace-effect fabric produced on a warp-knitting machine.

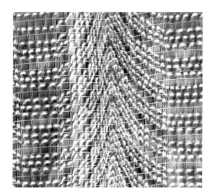

REPP SILK

Repp cloth is possibly a corruption of rib because it is woven in fine cords or ribs across the width of the piece.

RESIST-DYEING

A method of dyeing textiles to create pattern. Various methods of resist-dyeing can be used to prevent the dye from reaching all the cloth. The most common include the application of wax, the use of some type of paste and mechanical resists that manipulate the cloth, such as tying or stitching.

ROCAILLE BEAD

Also called seed beads because of their size and shape, the small, round glass beads are even in size and dual-coloured. The versatile reflection between rocaille beads of the same colour creates a multi-faceted effect.

SATEEN

Sateen is made from cotton or rayon that is usually mercerized to a satin-like finish. It is not as strong as satin because it is woven with four threads over and one under (as opposed to the traditional one over, one under). This gives a softer feel to the fabric.

SATIN

Densely woven silk with a smooth surface that reflects the light.

SATIN STITCH

Satin stitch, also known as damask stitch, is a series of flat stitches used to completely cover a section of the base fabric or as an outline to attach appliqués to the ground fabric.

SCHIFFLI (SWISS EMBRIODERY)

Isaac Groebli of Switzerland invented the first schiffli embroidery machine in 1863, utilizing the combination of a continuously threaded needle and a shuttle containing a bobbin of thread. The shuttle itself looked similar to the hull of a sailboat, hence the name 'schiffli' (*schiffli* means 'little boat' in Swiss German). In the process, the fabric is moved in front of a bank of a multi-head embroidery machine; the ensuing negative space is removed by a laser.

SCRAFFITI

In this surface treatment, a dark surface that has been coated with another colour is made to reappear in the form of lines, or stripes, by scratching away the differently coloured overpainting.

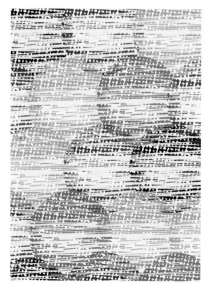

SCREEN-PRINTING

A laborious and handcrafted process, screen-printing is a technique that uses a woven mesh to support an ink-blocking stencil. The attached stencil forms open areas of mesh that transfer dyes to the fabric. A squeegee is moved across the screen stencil, forcing the pigment through the mesh openings. Each colour requires a separate screen.

SCROLLWORK

A decorative flourish featuring circular motifs or spirals, scrollwork resembles the edge-on view of a rolled-up parchment scroll.

SELVEDGE

This term is used to describe the self-finished edges of fabric. In woven fabric, selvedges are the edges that run parallel to the warp (the longitudinal threads that run the entire length of the fabric), and they are created by the weft thread looping back at the end of each row to form a secure edge.

SHIBORI

Shibori describes a variety of ways of embellishing textiles by shaping cloth using binding, knotting, stitching, folding, twisting or compressing and securing it before dyeing. The word comes from the Japanese verb root *shiboru*, meaning 'to wring, squeeze or press'. Each method is used to achieve a certain result, but also chosen to work in harmony with the type of cloth. Therefore, the technique utilized in shibori depends not only on the desired pattern, but also on the characteristics of the cloth being dyed. Different techniques can be used in conjunction with one another to achieve more elaborate results.

SHISHEH OR ABHLA BHARAT EMBROIDERY

A type of embroidery that attaches small pieces of mirrored reflective metal to fabric on a base cloth. It originated in 17th-century India and is found today in the indigenous textiles of Iran, India, Pakistan, Afghanistan, China and Indonesia. Traditionally, shisheh (meaning 'glass' in Persian) work was done using mica, but beetle, tin, silver and coins were not uncommon depending on the region. These were later replaced by glass that was blown into large, thin bubbles and broken into small pieces with a convex curve. This form of embroidery work is now most common on the Indian subcontinent.

SHOT EFFECT

The visual property of shot fabrics is defined as a *cangiante* (iridescent) effect, i.e. a slight shift in viewing position or a movement of the cloth results in significant colour changes.

SILK

Silk is a natural protein fibre. The best-known type of silk is obtained from cocoons made by the larvae of the mulberry silkworm, *Bombyx mori*, reared in captivity. Silk's unique lustre is due to the filament being the finest of all natural fibres. Despite its delicacy, it is extremely strong.

SLUB YARN

Slub yarn is spun with some sections along the yarn being thicker than others, thus producing an irregular appearance in the finished cloth. The thick sections are known as slubs.

SOUTACHE

Soutache is narrow, flat, decorative braid, traditionally woven from metallic bullion thread, silk or a blend of silk and wool. It is used in the trimming of drapery and clothing to conceal a seam. In the 20th century, soutache began to be woven in rayon and other synthetic fibres.

SPACE-DYEING

The creation of multi-colour yarns using applications of various colourants at intervals along a yarn. Space-dyeing produces a random rainbow effect.

STOCKING STITCH

A pattern of stitches in knitting consisting of alternate rows of plain and purl stitch. Its name derives from its use in hosiery.

TABBY WEAVE

A weave in which the filling threads and the warp threads interlace alternately, forming a chequerboard pattern. It is also called plain weave, linen weave or taffeta weave, and is strong and hard wearing.

TAMBOUR BEADING

Tambour work reputedly arrived in France in the 1720s from China. The technique requires the fabric to be stretched tight on a frame and a tambour hook is used to make a chain stitch. The hook is held on top of the frame with the threaded beads or sequins underneath.

TANA LAWN

A lightweight cotton printed fabric with a fine thread count named after Lake Tana in Sudan, which initially supplied the yarn.

TULLE

A sheer fabric with a mesh like structure creating very fine hexagonal holes. Tulle may be produced in silk, nylon or rayon and it is also known as net, illusion or maline.

TUSSAH SILK

Shantung is a plain silk woven from a tussah silk thread. This has an irregular quality, created during the spinning process, which forms a slub in the fabric as it is woven.

VERMICELLI WORK

A surface embroidery stitch formed from a continuous thread that meanders around the base cloth, this technique is so called because it resembles vermicelli (very fine spaghetti). It is also sometimes referred to as 'Cornelly couching'.

VOILE

A thin, plain-weave sheer fabric (from the French *voile*, meaning 'veil').

WARPING AND WEAVING

Woven cloth is produced on a loom. Weaving starts with the laying out of the warp thread, which runs vertically from the top to the bottom of the fabric in a predetermined pattern. The number of threads varies with the fineness of the yarn and the density of the cloth. The weave begins with the introduction of the weft yarn, which runs horizontally across the cloth, again laid out in a way predetermined by the designer. The shuttle is a device that carries the weft threads across the warp. There are many types of woven cloth.

WHOLEGARMENT® KNITTING

The introduction of Wholegarment® Shima Seiki machines has added a new genre of equipment to traditional knitted construction processes. The two major manufacturers of flat knitting machines are Stoll of Germany and Shima Seiki of Japan. Both companies have developed CAD pattern-generating systems linked to machine production. Electronic control has resulted in the easy manufacture of complex and sophisticated patterning and shaping, which previously were labour-intensive and expensive processes.

PHOTO CREDITS

The author and publisher would like to thank the designers, studios, labels and photographers for their kind permission to reproduce the images in this book. Every effort has been made to seek permission to reproduce these images. Any omissions or errors are entirely unintentional and can be corrected in future editions.

t = top; **tr** = top right; **r** = right; **br** = bottom right; **b** = bottom; **bl** = bottom left; **l** = left; **tl** = top left; **c** = centre

INDEX

ACKNOWLEDGMENTS

My grateful thanks to Tristan de Lancey and Jon Crabb at Thames & Hudson; Rebecca Gee, Tzortzis Rallis, Simon Pask and Florence Welby.

I would also like to thank the following: Adam Read of The Colorfield; Alexandra Loginova at David Koma; Alison Smart of R. A. Smart; Alyssa Wood at Louise Goldin; Ann Louise Roswald; Anna Buruma at Liberty London; Anthony Cox, Sarah Reynolds and Lok Wong at Megan Park; Antony Baker at Sophia Kokosalaki; Antony Waller at Bora Aksu; Beth Gilderoy and Rachel Storey at Barbour; Beth Richmond; Betty Jackson; Bruce Oldfield; Bruno Basso and Christopher Brooke of Basso & Brooke; C. J. B. Mason and Kate Knight of Cluny Lace; Carlo Volpi; Caroline Adams, Holly Robinson and Sarah Croll at The Communications Store; Caroline Forster and Miriam Ruthemann of Forster Rohner; Charlotte Taylor; Christopher Kane; David Koma; Dee Carpenter; Denis James and Frances Yvette of Insideout; Elizabeth Burns at Hussein Chalayan; Ellie Hipkin of Freyelli; Emma Hubbard at Matthew Williamson; Eloise Hautcoer at Starworks; Gemma Smith at Linton Tweeds; Gerard Wilson at Peter Jensen; Giles Deacon; Hannah George at Holly Fulton; Hannah Lyden-Vieten at Betty Jackson; Heather Snowden at Bruce Oldfield; Helen Turner; Henry Holland; Holly Fulton; Hussein Chalayan; Inès Michelet and Géraldine de La Brosse at Antik Batik; James Long; Jackie Turner at John Smedley; Jasmine Chan at Jonathan Saunders; Jenny Stewart at Johnstons of Elgin; Jerome Gautier at Dior; Jessica Jane at Hand & Lock; John Angus; Jonathan Saunders; Joseph Altuzarra; Juliet Bailey and Franki Brewer of Dash and Miller; Julie Brøgger at Preen by Thornton Bregazzi; Julius Walters of Stephen Walters Ltd; Justin Thornton and Thea Bregazzi of Preen by Thornton Bregazzi; Karen Nicol; Kate Dooley at Giles; Kazuhiro Ueno and Gaku Masui of Nuno Corporation; Kirsty McDougall of Dashing Tweeds; Jaqui Lewis of Lewis and Lewis Design; Libby Haan and Meredith de Blois at Haan Projects; Liz Roscoe at Modus Publicity; Louise Goldin; Louise Gray; Lu Jeffery; Maarit Heikkilä and Sanna-Kaisa Niikko at Marimekko; Mark Eley and Wakako Kishimoto of Eley Kishimoto; Mary Katrantzou; Matthew Williamson; Megan Park; Melissa Williams at Zandra Rhodes; Michael van der Ham; Natasha Surguladze of Tata Naka; Patricia Conway; Patricia Voto and Jodie Chan at Altuzarra; Paul Smith; Paul Vogel; Peter Jensen; Phillip and Nicole de Leon of Alexander Henry Fabrics; Raf Simons of Dior; Ruth Davis at Eley Kishimoto; Sam Twyford at James Long; Sophia Kokosalaki; Susan Lager and Mary-Ann Dunkley at Paul Smith; Thakoon Panichgul; Tove Westling at Varg Ltd; Val Furphy and Ian Simpson of Furphy Simpson; Vicki Murdoch of Silken Favours; Yaelle Caplan of Yaelle; Yumiko Hayashi at Sonia Rykiel; Zandra Rhodes; Zara Siddiqui-Lester of The Colour Union.

Finally I would most particularly like to thank Allan Hutchings for his wonderful photography.